CRYSTALS
AND THEIR USE

OF READER INTEREST:

"The Magic of Minerals" by Page Bryant

"Planetary Influences and Therapeutic Uses of Precious Stones" by George F. Kunz

"Man, Minerals and Masters" by Dr. Charles W. Littlefield

CRYSTALS
AND THEIR USE

A STUDY OF AT-ONE-MENT
WITH THE MINERAL KINGDOM

By Page Bryant

**Channeled From
Albion**

Illustrations By Scott Guynup

**Sun Books
Sun Publishing Company
Santa Fe, N.M.**

First Printing.................1984 Sep
Second Printing...............1985 Mar
Third Printing................1985 Jul
Fourth Printing...............1985 Sep
Fifth Printing................1985 Nov
Sixth Printing................1986 Aug
Seventh Printing..............1986 Oct
Eighth Printing...............1987 Mar
Ninth Printing................1987 Jul
Tenth Printing................1987 Oct
Eleventh Printing.............1993 Aug

Sun Books
Sun Publishing Company
Santa Fe, N.M.

ISBN: 0-89540-151-7

Printed in the United States of America

For Helaine

ACKNOWLEDGEMENTS

A special thanks must go to Lorraine Walton for her help in making this little booklet a reality. I also wish to thank Helaine M. McLain, Scott Guynup, and all the members of the Monday night Albion class, who have used the material since it was first channeled.

TABLE OF CONTENTS

PREFACE

Since ancient times, man has been interested in the use of gems, herbs, metals, and stones as a tool for healing and/or spiritual growth. Of all these, *crystallomancy,* the use of a crystal for divination, certainly has remained one of the most popular.

There seems to be a revival of interest in the use of crystals for various metaphysical purposes. I became aware of the broad interest about two years ago and hoped that my Teacher, Albion, would make comment on them at sometime. I heard of the information that was being taught by various teachers and medicine people, in particular, from Harley Swiftdeer (a Cherokee medicineman.) His teachings refer to the use of the mineral as White Crystal Medicine.

Crystal is a term of perfection. The Greeks gave it its name. They called this mineral *krystallos* due to its appearance. The word *krystallos* means "ice." Crystals have always been prized for their regularity of form and for their transparency. All minerals with these qualities are considered crystals. These minerals can be found all over the world , and are usually found in groups. It is rare that one finds single crystals.

Seven has long been considered a sacred or mystical number by the Ancients. It is the number attributed to order out of chaos. Looking at the shape of a crystal, we find that it is divided into seven lattice systems. They are the cubic, hexagonal, trigonal, tetragonal, orthorhombic, monoclinic, and triclinic.

When Albion channeled this information, he said that many people are incarnating today who have a memory of using crystals for various purposes in the past . . . in other lives. We are all familiar with the stories about the Atlanteans and their use of crystals as batteries to store power. Much about this is to be found in the Edgar Cayce material. The "remembering" that is going on gives us another chance to learn the proper use of the mineral kingdom and the energies that it has to share with mankind. One of the memories that has brought archaic knowledge once again to the surface is the use of crystals, quartz crystals for various purposes concerning healing, time travel, and aura balancing.

This material is designed to give you insight as to the proper use and care of the crystal, as well as information concerning the use of the amethyst. Correct use of the crystal creates at-one-ment between the mineral and the human kingdoms and their unique types of consciousness. It is hoped that the contents of this book will bring you positive results. The class to which this information was originally taught has experimented with this concept and has had good results. Your at-one-ment with the mineral kingdom will, hopefully, be as successful.

Page Bryant

Chapter 1
MINERAL
CONSCIOUSNESS

The consciousness of all kingdoms is a mechanism of awareness that comes directly from the Mind of God. Choosing the word mechanism implies a type of computer or a piece of machinery whose total purpose is to calculate what it encounters within any dimension of time, space, or circumstance. The mechanism of consciousness, having its origin in Divine Thought, is a response to stimuli. Whether the stimuli come from objective forces, other bodies, or from within the soul consciousness itself, it is not responded to until consciousness is employed.

It can also be said that consciousness has, as a part of its purpose, to synchronize vibrations. This could lead to the next step, that consciousness can and does synthesize experiences. Synchronicity and synthesis are two very important activities of consciousness. If consciousness were simply "being aware", it would not provide a broad enough spectrum of understanding, since consciousness must evolve into its ultimate state of being able to synchronize the vibrations it encounters as well as synthesize its experiences. So, just "being aware" overlooks the inner workings of consciousness and, most importantly, its evolutionary process. The events, thoughts, and feelings that are experienced as earthly living would be detached and isolated units of stimuli were it not for the consciousness that brings them together into associated thought and thus into a synthesis of understanding.

As with all life forms, the bodies within the mineral kingdom are composed of atoms, and each of these atoms had a consciousness within itself long before it became coagulated into a mineral. So, each atom that composes a crystal, for example, has a consciousness of its own and thus can respond to stimuli, can be aware, and can synthesize the vibrations it encounters as well as synchronize. The subatomic particles of the atoms that would eventually comprise the mineral kingdom were ejected into manifestation at the very beginning of Creation. After these atoms were created, they wandered about rather aimlessly until the infant atoms were able to vibrate and thus send a telepathic signal in that vibration to other atoms of the same sort, since the atoms that compose every form of matter that will ever exist were composed at that moment of Creation. Once the telepathic signals or vibrations of the atoms were set up, then the long process of joining forces to become plant, mineral, animal, or human began to take place.

The first form of reality or matter, on this planet

or other celestial bodies was mineral. The mineral kingdom coagulates and attracts atoms of its own kind, and is concerned only with the building of form. Minerals are not concerned with intellect or emotion; they are concerned only with the building of form. Basic research will soon determine that the complexity of form-building within the mineral kingdom is quite astounding. In addition to the observable physical form of minerals there are various geometrical designs involving the inner form structures. For example, within the crystal, the most highly-evolved member of the mineral kingdom, there are seven specific geometrical designs that are built one upon the other, one leading to another.

Consciousness within the mineral kingdom can be compared to a trance-like state in human consciousness. There is no degree of self-awareness in the mineral kingdom, only the purpose of creating and building form. It is that form which composes our planet Earth and every single other body that exists in the solar system if, indeed, it is part of the world of matter.

Although there is no intelligence or *self*-awareness (in the human sense) in the mineral kingdom, it is still possible for humans to influence or harm its members. This is accomplished by interrupting the process of form-building, the karmic responsibility of the mineral kingdom. Mankind dynamites the

13

side of a mountain to build a road, and removes or re-forms stones to construct homes and fences. He interrupts the natural process of form-building to build his own forms.

It is incorrect to assume automatically that as evolution proceeds, consciousness gets better and things become more highly evolved. Rather, evolution simply determines the degree or amount of consciousness that is involved. For example, a member of the animal kingdom has a more intense, more solid degree of consciousness than a mineral, but it would not be correct to say that one is more evolved than the other. The misunderstanding that one type of consciousness is more spiritual, intelligent, or highly-evolved than another is the major factor involved in the separation and superiority that humans feel toward all the other kingdoms of life. Minerals, plants, and animals have been on earth longer than mankind. Perhaps man should contemplate how time has enhanced each of these types of consciousness.

In the mineral kingdom, as with all kingdoms, each atom is composed of individual microscopic particles of existence; and each particle has consciousness. Each of those particles joins together to create an atom, and each atom joins to create the body or form. Thus, there exists consciousness within each particle and fiber of the total structure. Since each sub-atomic particle has consciousness, then it is also endowed with the Divine Heritage of consciousness, free will.

Through the force of free will, the sub-atomic particles come together to create form. The particles that have come together to comprise a mineral, such as the crystal, have only one motive for being and that is to create form, which is the first manifestation. It is the first task of consciousness to create form, nothing more and nothing less. Their basic inherent quality, the creation of form, follows the sub-atomic particles throughout eternity.

Every other kingdom of existence is composed of recycled particles that have the knowledge and the desire to create form. If this were not so, humans could have no bodies, and plants and animals would have no vehicle of expression. So, the primary function of consciousness is constructive, creative; and form is the result. Consciousness is the inside of the potential of reality, and the mineral kingdom is its first manifestation.

The free will of each kingdom has been, at times, interrupted by another kingdom. The free will of the choice of behavior and manifestation of that kingdom, as a result, has been taken over by another kingdom of life. This type of imposition can be karmically good or bad. If a man pulls a carrot from the ground to nourish his body, it allows the plant kingdom to contribute its life force to the survival and perpetuation of the human kingdom, the imposing kingdom. On the other hand, if a man snatches a carrot from the earth and uses it to decorate his table as part of a centerpiece, he has treated that kingdom with disrespect by not allowing it to make the type of contribution singular to its consciousness.

Minerals, particularly crystals, with their form-building consciousness, can be used in healing, in re-forming manifestation. To re-shape a crystal and wear it upon a chain around one's neck as ornamentation is blasphemy toward the mineral kingdom. A natural crystal used for healing, however, interrupts the free will of the mineral kingdom for the assistance of the human kingdom, a proper and karmically positive sacrifice and task. Correct use of the crystal creates at-one-ment between the mineral and human kingdoms and their unique types of consciousness

Chapter 2
CRYSTALS AND
THEIR USE—PART 1

We feel that it is time to share information that has a great bearing on this particular time of mankind's evolution upon the planet Earth. There has been information that has been channeled in the past that has concerned the Earth and the changes that she approaches that will, in turn, affect all of the life forms upon her. We want to impress upon you that these changes are natural and necessary, and they have occurred many times in the past. They are a part of the Divine Plan. It so happens that oftentimes the prophecies tend to label the Earth changes as negative, and this can cause you to lose the greatest lesson of all, which is that periods of Earth changes are a process that is involved with the planet going through its own phases of evolution and initiation.

Each time there approaches a period of change, it also coincides, for the most part, with the changing of an Age. When this occurs, there is always a struggle with the old Age and its energies, all of its established teachings, its society and governmental functions, to bombard or otherwise create a barrier towards the incoming Age. It is like a struggle for survival and we see this in operation at this point in time with the Piscean Age trying to withstand the Aquarian energies that have been pushing in gradually since the end of the last century. This is a slow process, but a steady one.

As the "new age" advances, there will be periods of time that the new energies will be more apparent and even seem stronger than those of the existing Age. This can cause feelings and events of social and political, even religious unrest, and also give the people that are incarnate during such a time feelings of emotional, mental, and spiritual insecurity. At such times, it becomes a natural tendency for man to reach back into his subconscious mind and remember various instruments, tools, theories, and practices that he has used and known before. Oftentimes there will be those that will retrieve memories and practices from lifetimes that they have lived during other periods of history. Whether or not one remembers what period of time or the location in which they lived is not really that important. Most of the time, such information, particularly regarding the location and period of time, will be apparent. This is true with the reemergence of the use of pyramid energy, which was known and practiced long ago by the ancient Egyptians and even as far back as the Atlanteans. It is important to note that many of the occult practices that are being used today are memories of techniques that have been used during other lifetimes, especially during the time of the now lost Atlantis.

Time can erase the physical remnants of whole civilizations, but it cannot erase the memories of the men and women who might have lived there in ancient times. Many medical breakthroughs and other scientific successes have come through to modern man through the memory of others. There are inventions that are brought through in this manner, as well. The automobile, the battery, and even airplanes, are prime examples of such inventions that seem to belong only to modern science and technology when, in fact, they do not. This sort of ability seems to become more prevalent when we approach periods of great changes and we will see evidence of this in the future. We should watch, in particular, the field of medical science, for with the birth of the Holistic approach to living, it has brought to the surface much memory, which has been used and will be used more and more in the future. We will see more use of "psychic" healing. It has also been referred to as magnetic healing, psychic or etheric surgery, and incorporates the ancient knowledge of the "science of breath". These are all indicative of ancient capabilities reborn into modern society. As we have seen, these capabilities may seem unorthodox and are often rejected by the scientific community. But, this is the most prominent route to discovery, and it will continue to be evident.

One of the things that you can watch for in the future that will be a use of a past capability reemerging into modern life, is the use of sound currents for repairing the physical body. You will see clinics and research centers spring up all over the free world. Sound will also be used for the treatment of the mental body of man and also to stimulate his psyche. Sound will be used to help restore wasted energies in the physical self. The initial activity of this sort will come from the country of England and will quickly spread over the globe. There are also entities who are coming forward who will remember symbols that were of great significance to religious and philosophical organizations from the past, and also rituals that were designed to bring about specific information and vibrations which will be remembered and integrated again into our society. This will bring mankind into a closer understanding and relationship with Deity and into a greater discovery of the human soul. This is why there are so many groups that are evolving based upon metaphysical concepts and which hold a belief in the lifestyle and history of past cultures such as the Mayans, the Egyptians, and the Atlanteans.

One of the memories that has brought archaic knowledge once again to the surface is the use of crystals, quartz crystals, for various purposes to do with healing, time travel, and aura balancing. This "memory" is re-emerging with individuals that are leaders of groups designed to study the ways of the Native Americans through self-development and awareness groups, and other special interest groups that are involved with the broad spectrum of New Age study.

There is wisdom connected with the crystal, and in order to fully understand it, let us first consider that there are four major kingdoms of life living upon the Earth. The majority of people do not readily relate to any spiritual or divine implications that exist within any of those kingdoms except for their human brothers and sisters. Most do not consider, for example, any spiritual or psychic capabilities of a rock or a tree. But, within the mineral kingdom, to which the crystal belongs, there are atoms of a like nature that are drawn together to create forms. This is the principle that separates a diamond from a ruby, or a grain of sand from a boulder or sedimentary rock. As forms, these minerals tend to create a sort of "personality" or egoic-like structure. This can be experienced by holding a diamond in one hand and a jasper stone in the other. You will sense that each of these objects vibrates differently, thus shedding a different energy which can be detected. Although they are obviously different in the physical sense, it is also true that they differ in terms or their spiritual purpose and usefulness to the other kingdoms of life.

Quartz is a mineral that is transparent and has

geometric regularity. Crystal is a term of perfection. The Greeks gave it its name. They called this mineral krystallos due to its appearance. The word krystallos means "ice." It is the structure of the substance, the way in which its external faces are shaped and related to one another, which defines it as a crystal. It is also important to note that the crystal has symmetry. Any crystal can be rotated about a number of different axes in such a way that the same configuration of faces appears more than once during the course of that rotation. These are the axes of symmetry. There are also planes of symmetry that would permit one to cut a crystal in half, and each half would reflect the other perfectly.There is also a center of symmetry in which the face of the crystal has a similar face lying parallel to it on the other side of the mineral. It is rare that one finds single crystals, for they usually occur in groups which have developed together in rock fissures, on flat surfaces known as druses, or in cavities known as geodes.

When the word crystal is spoken, it will often invoke a memory within the consciousness of those who have worked with crystals in the past. This is seen often with collectors and with those who work with crystals for various purposes. The atoms that make up the body of this mineral are "magnetic" in their vibration (as it is sensed by the psychic abilities) and therefore, they have the ability to attract and magnetize energies and forces. The crystal will or can draw vibrations also from other life forms. It can equally reach into the astral plane and other dimensions, as well, and draw energies from those levels. This is so, for the crystal is one of the few life forms upon the planet that has the ability to penetrate from one dimension of existence into another. Were you to view the crystal with clairvoyant sight, you would see that there is somewhat of a haze around it, for the astral body of the crystal exists on the periphery, within the auric field. It is this astral body that has the attracting power. The physical body of the crystal simply acts as a battery and will store what has been attracted.

This particular form of practice is now a very important tool that will become more and more common to the masses as time goes on. There will be more information that will be revealed in the future and you should keep in mind that the information could vary considerably from channel to channel. This is due to the fact that they were used in various ways by several civilizations during the Atlantean era and for specific and sometimes varied purposes.

There are three primary purposes that crystals can and are being used for at this time. In order to better understand, I will divide the use of crystals into categories, and I will discuss each one and its use.

First of all, "chakra" crystals. These crystals can be used or programmed to balance the seven sacred centers in the human body. As they are held to the centers in question, they will absorb negative energy in order to create a balance. They can also release energy into the chakras that has been stored in the mineral prior to your work. This can be administered by yourself or by another person, with your permission, of course.

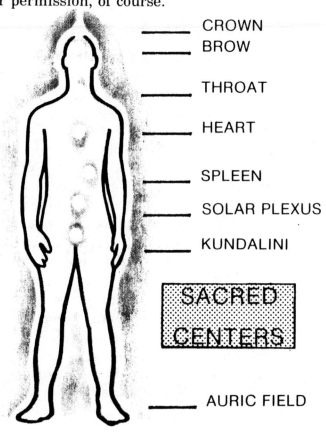

CROWN
BROW

THROAT

HEART

SPLEEN

SOLAR PLEXUS

KUNDALINI

SACRED CENTERS

AURIC FIELD

There should be seven crystals chosen for this purpose and they should each weigh at least eight ounces. These crystals should be used for no other purpose. The reason for the size is two-fold. First, they can be easily held in your hand if they are large and also, they can store large quantities of energies that are extracted from or that need to be put into the chakra areas.

REMEMBER: EACH CHAKRA CRYSTAL
SHOULD WEIGH 8 OUNCES OR MORE!

THE KUNDALINI CRYSTAL

BURY THE CRYSTAL IN THE EARTH
FOR AT LEAST 24 HOURS PRIOR TO USE!

THE CRYSTAL ABSORBS
THE EARTH'S MAGNETISM

The crystal used for restoring balance to and energizing the anal chakra (the Kundalini), should be buried in the ground for at least a twenty-four hour period. This is so that it can absorb the magnetism of the Earth which can be used to stimulate and balance the "serpent fire" in the shaft of the spine. Oftentimes there are pains in the spine and all sorts of imbalances of the chemical sense in the Kundalini. It is very important to keep this chakra in as perfect a state as possible, and the crystal is quite useful in this manner.

THE
SOLAR PLEXUS CRYSTAL

SOAK CRYSTAL IN PURIFIED OR DISTILLED WATER PRIOR TO USE

DISTILLED WATER

The crystal used for the solar plexus chakra should be soaked in purified or distilled water for a short period of time prior to use. The solar plexus is closely associated with the emotional or astral body and thus long related to the element of water. Holding the crystal to this center can still the churning that often goes on and bring a balance to the feelings one might be experiencing. Again, remember, a crystal of eight ounces must be used to serve this purpose sufficiently.

THE SPLEEN CRYSTAL

THE COLOR ORANGE IS ASSOCIATED WITH THE SPLEEN CHAKRA

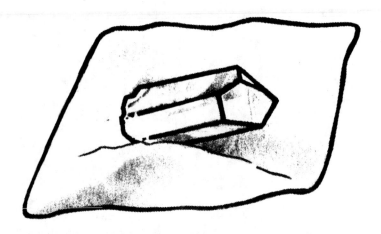

Choose a crystal that will be touched to the spleen center. This center is the purifier of the bodies and it can take the toxins out of the etheric body which, in itself, is a balancing effect. This crystal should be stored in an orange container or piece of fabric. This is the color that the Ancient Wisdoms associated with this center.

THE HEART CRYSTAL

ALWAYS STORE THIS CRYSTAL IN AN AIR-TIGHT CONTAINER

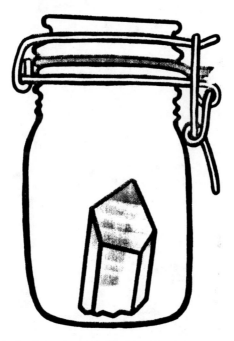

The heart chakra is a delicate center, one that can be thrown off balance very easily. A crystal that is chosen for working on this center should be 8 to 10 ounces in weight. It is touched lightly to the heart center and after use should be stored in some sort of air-tight container.

THE THROAT, BROW, AND CROWN CRYSTALS

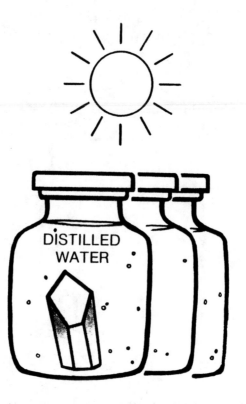

EXPOSE THESE CRYSTALS TO SUN-LIGHT
REGULARLY

The throat and brow chakra crystals should also be purified with water. They can be approximately the same size as the others and they need to be exposed to sunlight regularly. So, also, should the crown chakra crystal, for the energies of prana in the sun's rays are absorbed and, in turn, released into the "breath of life" force, and it is pure light. It is prana.

I suggest that the chakras, like the physical body, should be brought into balance once a day. Use your own chakra crystals only on yourself. If you are going to work on others, you should have another set of seven crystals for that purpose and they should be carefully drained of all energy absorbed after the treatment by the use of water, and in the case of the one that is to be buried in the earth, it should be reburied each time.

In regards to the chakra crystals and their effect in balancing the auric field or energy field around your body, remember that each chakra should have its own crystal and that they should not be mixed up. Perhaps you would want to label your minerals in some way or buy them in different shapes so that keeping them separate would not be difficult. You might consider labeling the jars or containers that they will be kept in since they can be used time and time again. If you were to use the wrong crystal on the wrong center, that could cause a problem. Let me explain.

If you were to use the crystal that you have designated for the Kundalini center on the solar plexus, you would cause problems for yourself. The Kundalini crystal is used for raising and lowering the energies that are active and present in this center and this center is electrical in its nature. If you were to work on the solar plexus with it, you would short-circuit the emotional or astral body due to placing electrical and expanding energies into a magnetic and receptive center. Think carefully about this. You could harm your etheric body. It could manifest by lack of control of your emotions and definitely an intensifying of the emotional reactions to various circumstances in your life. This is an obvious imbalance. Also, if you were to use the Kundalini crystal on the heart center, another magnetic opening, you could cause damage to the love center and thus have difficulties with projection and reception and understanding of love and your ability to deal with that all-important emotional and spiritual matter.

MEDITATION CRYSTALS

Another sort of crystal that is useful for balancing purposes, but more on a mental and spiritual level, is the meditation crystal. This can be a crystal of any size and, I might add, that in choosing any of these minerals to work with you should feel "drawn" to the proper crystal for your use. In turn, you will have allowed the energy of that particular crystal to come to you, rather than you being in total control of the choices.

During quiet moments of thought and contemplation, hold the meditation crystal that you have selected. Holding it in your hands, you will find that it will stir and activate your thought processes. However, as opposed to thoughts of material or emotional matters, these thoughts that come up are apt to be ones of the past ... such as past lives, the past in this life and such thoughts that will activate certain of your chakras. You will also recall certain instances that are important to your growth and understanding ....instances that occurred long ago but that have still yet to be resolved in your own mind. The crystal will help the subconscious in formulating and storing the thoughts received and in holding them for future reference and use. This is a thought-form building process and it is very useful with those of you who use meditation as a tool or method of self-discovery and development. It is as if the crystal becomes a bit of an Akashic Record of its own accord and as these revelations and positive thoughts come through in meditation, they can be stored and used during other times.

During everyday living, when there is some sort of erratic energy going on within you or around you, or you perhaps have to contend with depression or grief or anger, you might pick up the meditation crystal that you have been storing with calming thoughts and vibrations and it can serve as a sort of tranquilizer by releasing thoughts that are more inspired and certainly more controlled. If people would program a crystal for this use, there would certainly be less use for chemicals.

This is the same principle that is used by some cultures in using what is known as the "worry" stone. Here we find an ordinary stone being rubbed, and therefore programmed with one's "worry" thoughts and anxieties.

This is a positive and therapeutic transaction. It also serves to bring one into a closer relationship and understanding of the mineral kingdom of life.

SOUND CRYSTALS

Another sort of crystal that we wish to discuss we elect to call the sound crystal. To do so, we don't need to go into a lengthy discussion of sound currents scientifically, but it is of importance to note that these currents can be utilized for positive or negative purposes. Which it will be will totally depend on the motivation of the user. The Soviet and the United States governments have already experimented with the use of sound currents, although the real thrust of the work has been kept a closely guarded secret. This same sort of use of sound currents is part of the reason Atlantis does not now exist. Sound was part of the triggering mechanism for the Earth changes that took place upon that continent many years ago. Experiments backfired and they did so due to the negative use of an occult power.

When you choose your sound crystal, it should be used and touched only by yourself. This crystal is a most interesting one and one whose use can be tested for its validity. You must choose the mineral and then implant within it a suggestion as to its purpose. Then, the crystal can be taken to concerts, placed in a room where there is conversation, in the presence of your stereo or any other circumstance or location where you are interested in the sound energies that are or will be taking place. You must carry it and place it there. Once it is there, you may leave it and retrieve it later. It will hold musical currents, voices of individuals, even the vibrations of certain locations on or within the Earth. This sort of crystal is especially useful to those who are interested in knowing the solidity and therefore the safety of certain Earth areas in respect to the possibility of seismic activity. Such activity puts out sound and it can be detected and stored by your crystal. Virtually any object, person, or phenomena that generates vibrations, which in turn project sound energies, can be apprehended and captured by this crystal. It will also apprehend sound waves that might only be audible to the "psychic" ear, and as you touch it again, it will transmit, telepathically, the information that it has stored. It can be used as an excellent dowsing instrument, for if you place it in an area where you feel there might be water, it can record the sound of the running liquid. Also, psychometry, which is the belief that an object retains the vibrations of its history, is the same type of principle that is involved with the sound crystals.

The sound crystal should be kept in water at all times that it is not in use. Tap water will do just fine. Sound crystals can be cleansed by passing them through a small flame, such as a lighted candle, or by submerging them in a saline solution, preferably sea water.

At this point in the channeling session, there were questions that were posed to the Teacher. A student wanted to know if you should bury the crystal in the earth itself or would putting it in a pot of earth be just as good. The answer was empahtic that one should bury the crystal in the earth so it can get the full benefit of the vibration of the planet as a whole. Another question had to do with the length of time that one of the charkra crystals should be held to the chakra itself. Twenty or thirty seconds was the time given. It was also stressed that the heart crystal should not be used for the spleen, and so forth. Once a crystal has been chosen for a specific center, it should only be used on that center each time.

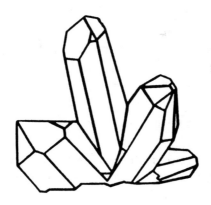

Chapter 3
CRYSTALS AND THEIR USE—PART II

The purpose of this chapter is to share further information that came through the Teacher concerning crystals and their use for various psychic and spiritual tasks.

The Teacher indicated during this part of the study that there are people who are living on the Earth right now that have used many different methods of healing, and some of these techniques were used in other lives. He suggested that the use of the crystals will not hinder, but enhance, one's healing abilities. It is a natural part of the function of the subconscious mind that when there is a physical object to hold in your hand, and that object can be used for helping with the healing, there is a stronger connection made, a stronger circuit for the healing energies to travel. The use of the crystal improves concentration.

Many crystals of all sizes can be used for healing. It is not necessary that they be very large, just large enough for you to hold onto. Even a sliver will do. It would also be wise for you to understand the nature of the problem within yourself or the other person that you are dealing with. Is the problem just a physical one? Remember, many illnesses are not physical in their origin. Although it is true that the crystal's energy does affect the etheric and astral bodies, it is for the purpose of healing the physical self. When you have discerned that the problem in question is physical, then hold the crystal in your hands, preferably in the palm of the right hand, for this is the side of the body that emits a positive, male, and electrical current. The left side of the body emits a more magnetic and feminine, receptive type of energy. While you are holding the crystal in your hand, project your own thoughts of healing into the mineral in order to program it with the proper intentions. The crystal will receive and hold the thoughts that are implanted. Because the crystal has these unique properties, it becomes quite plain to see why there is such a thin line between black and white magic, for it could just as easily be used for ill intent. Misuse of crystals and other tools has been done in ancient times and there are those who would choose to use them for ill again. Motivation is the all-important key to the crystal's proper use.

As you instill your thoughts of healing into the crystal, instruct it to absorb all negativity and impurity from the body, that it should become perfect and healthy once again. Then place the crystal on the area of the body that is in need of healing. Leave it on the surface of the skin until you "sense" that it has remained long enough to release its healing rays. If you will hold your hand approximately an inch above the crystal itself, you will notice that it will seem to heat up and you will be able to feel the heat coming from the mineral. As long as it generates heat, it is still doing its work. Wait until you can no longer feel warmth coming from the crystal, and then remove it. Take it at once and bury it in the ground so that the toxins and negative energies will be released into the Earth. If there is more than one crystal that has been used, due to more than one part of the body that is in need of healing, bury them all. Once a healing crystal has been buried after being used on the body, leave it there. Never touch it again. It is the nature of the quartz mineral to be able to absorb, store, and, in turn, release energy.

Let us now go into a discussion of the use of crystals for balancing the aura. We shall go into this in greater detail than before. This particular information and form of practice is a very important tool and one that will become more important and more available to the masses. There will be more information that will be revealed through various channels. Also, it is important to keep in mind that through these different channels, the information will tend to be a bit different. This is due to the fact that the use of crystals was prominent during different civilizations during ancient times, and therefore used for different and varying purposes.

The use of the crystal that we would like to discuss concerns the balancing or healing of the emotional/astral body. So many of the ailments that man is faced with are due to imbalances within his emotional/astral self, and thus are based on feelings. The difference between an illness that is emotional and one that is physical in its origin is such a fine line that medical science has only begun to try to understand and treat such problems. Doctors are just now becoming aware of how an undernourished or overnourished emotional body can cause diseases that are common and readily identified, such as cancer. We live at a time when there are a lot of social, political, financial and religious conflicts to deal with. Illness that comes as a result of all this is more common than one might think. All of these pressures provide a climate for emotional and psychological insecurity which grows slowly but surely inside the human form. Psychiatry and psychology have begun to treat such problems, but there is still a long way to go. Various courses of self-development and self-awareness have been thriving worldwide as a result of the dawning of understanding that the state of the body is due to the state of the mind and emotions.

The method of using the crystals that we are about to discuss will go far in helping to balance the emotional astral bodies within man and this is our ultimate aim in sharing this information. It is a tedious process that was, in ancient times, practiced only by the Initiates.

First of all, choose two crystals. They may be of any size that you would like. One is to be designated to work with positive/electric polarities and the other with the negative/magnetic energies. In order to work with bringing balance to the astral self, it would be easier to work with this when the astral form is out of coincidence with the physical. This is so whether you are going to work on yourself or on another person. You can follow a very basic technique to project the astral body so that it can be worked with. This technique can be used on others, too.

Sit quietly in a place where you know that you will not be disturbed, preferably in a straight chair, not lying down. Before you go into deep meditation, sit in this chair and place both feet (bare) flat on the floor. You should rest both hands in your lap. Relax. Take one of the crystals, the one that is magnetic, and place it between your feet; place the electric crystal on the top of your head. Then, through affirmation and breathing, force the astral body out through the solar plexus. It will be as if the astral body is a filmy duplicate of the physical resting a short distance in front of the physical body. As the bodies move out of coincidence, you should feel a pull on the physical body or a "click" in the center of the head, between the ears. Both of these sensations are indicative of the astral body being out of coincidence with the physical form.

Next, in your thoughts, command the crystals to absorb the negative and toxic substances. This will rejuvenate the astral fibers and the aura will be cleansed. This may take some time, but when the astral body is cleared, you will feel a sense of lightness and refreshment in the solar plexus area. You might also experience an uplifting feeling. During the process you might re-live in your thoughts some negative experience from the past. This is a good indication that the crystals are doing their work. As each emotional experience clogging the astral body is cleared, your emotional reaction to the clearing could range from light to heavy. Some people experience tears and pain during the release. This is a good process for releasing a lot of surface emotional toxins.

After you have completed this process, spend a few moments to regroup your energies, and then place these crystals in salt water, preferably natural seawater. They should be stored there until their next use. This process could be done on a daily basis or as often as one feels such a need. It should be done after particularly strong emotional encounters or fears.

If you are going to use the process on another person, you should instruct them in the simple process of projecting their astral body, then you can proceed to place the crystals and use your own words and thoughts to clear their astral form. This is a similar process to healing with the laying on of hands in that you are working with a person's force field in order to instill positive and clear feelings and thoughts.

It is also important for us to note that if you are already working with some method of healing, the use of the crystals will not hinder that work. It should only serve to enhance it. Remember, the crystals do not generate the energy you are using, but absorb it and balance it. It is usually a good idea to program your crystals with the right hand and then place them on the body. It is also a good idea to re-program them from time to time.

If you would like to use the crystal for absentee healing, it can work well. You would need a full length photograph of the person, if possible, but an ordinary photo will do. Take a magnetic crystal and place it on the bottom of the picture; place an electric crystal on the top. Most photos will reveal the top of the head, and this is the most important part of the body to work with in this type of procedure. The same procedure can be followed as when you work with a person who is there with you. But, since the astral body should be distracted by you in this case, it is not a good idea to attempt to work to this extent without the knowledge and permission of the person involved. Also, correlating times for the healing to be done is a good idea whenever possible. After this healing process is achieved, whether in person or at a distance, the astral body (which is connected to the physical by a sort of umbilical cord) will snap back, thus bringing the astral body back into coincidence with the physical. Since the astral body will only need to be a few inches away from the physical for this process, there is very little danger of harm.

The only time that there might be potential danger would be with a person that is completely out of control of their emotional self, as with someone who is insane or recovering from a nervous breakdown. In these cases, avoid this method of healing entirely.

Not long after the previous information was channeled, there were additional comments that were shared concerning the use of crystals to cleanse the thoughts. That information, it was said, must be put to use before it could really have any impact at all upon one's consciousness. Perhaps that is true of all of the information regarding the use of crystals; and that should be borne in mind when any sort of practice is pursued with the hope of receiving maximum results. In the next section we will consider thought and how it accumulates in the consciousness.

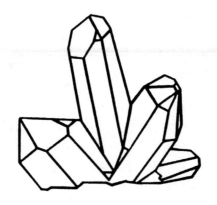

THOUGHT CLEANSING CRYSTALS

We are all thinkers. We have all heard the expression that "thoughts are things", and most of us strive to implement that truth into our everyday lives, trying to be cautious about the thoughts that we have, especially the ones that are fearful or negative, so that we do not manifest those fears and ill thought expressions into our physical lives. When a thought is created within the mind, it is impossible for that thought to go unvitalized. Once it has been given birth, that thought will go forth and bring about the conditions upon which it is based, causing thought to be the prime motivating force in our lives.

But, there is another activity of thought that must also be considered here, and that is that thoughts may also remain "trapped" within our consciousness and collect, one upon the other, forming fragments of both positive and negative ideas and concepts to remain stagnant in the mind. This can become a sort of "thought potpourri" that may have effects upon the mind, soul, and body with some devastating results.

It has been understood that thoughts are singular in their original nature, but through the electrical activity of impulses taking place inside the human brain, one thought will automatically associate itself with another through the memory, which tends to link thoughts together in chains. When a thought has been conceived within the mind, it is important that you understand that the life force instilled within it comes from the etheric and the astral bodies of man. For example, when an artist conceives an image of a painting that he wishes to do, that image may be an idea which is composed of many singular thoughts. It is like the many pieces of a puzzle which, when placed upon canvas, forms the thoughts into a physical duplication. Such a product is the function of the astral or desire body inside of the painter to create his idea and make it a reality.

Now, let us consider another angle to the process that the artist must go through in order to do a painting. Let us say the artist does not immediately sit down and create the painting from his thoughts, but allows them to remain within his mind for several days or even months before, if ever, that image comes into manifestation. The thoughts are then stored in the memory bank as vitalized, living ideas. Then, through the course of living, the same artist (as all of us do) will have other thoughts that will accumulate, such as a trip that he has been wanting to take but hasn't, thoughts concerning health, chores, ideas and relationships with other people. All of these "living" thoughts that are not acted upon tend to build up. You can surely begin to see how crowded the consciousness can get, considering how much we think in a very short amount of time. Thoughts that have not been acted upon are thoughts that stagnate. This can be due to procrastination, forgetfulness, or even laziness. It can also be due to changing one's mind. Over a period of many years, thoughts that are collecting in the memory and consciousness can cause one to live in the past, get hung-up and confused, be critical of oneself and a myriad of other emotional and mental frustrations. When these cluttered thought fragments begin to fester, they transform and affect our motivations, our feelings, and, most importantly of all, our normal process of thinking. They become emotional debris. Such thoughts can turn reality into fantasy or pure illusion.

When there is such a clog in our mental stream which, as we have seen, can affect our emotional, physical and even spiritual progress, something must be done in order to clear it away.

Let us consider those thoughts which are very positive in their nature, for they are assumed to be the best for us. Well, if positive thoughts are electrical in their type and they are not acted upon in some manner, they can become very dangerous to the Self, especially the physical and emotional Self, and one's life can become filled with a lot of good intentions that have stagnated! So, it can be said that thought of any sort which is not used becomes excess mental baggage, and is of no good value.

Quite the contrary, it can become destructive.

It becomes necessary, therefore, to devise a way to cleanse ourselves of excess thoughts that have built up within us. For such a task, let us once again consider crystals.

We have already explained that the quartz mineral has the capacity to be programmed as you would desire it to function. You are the programmer! The crystal can be programmed to absorb those excess thoughts and thus cleanse the consciousness.

Begin by selecting a crystal for this purpose of any size you desire. Thoughts may always be replaced as you begin to cleanse them. It will definitely call your attention to the nature of the dormant ideas, and this will serve as a good reminder to you as to what you have actually stored within you that has not been used. You might surprise yourself by working with this process and learning what you have been carrying around literally!

The amount of time spent on this project and the frequency of its use is a matter that is entirely dependent upon what each individual feels is correct. It is also important to note that as the crystal gathers and cleans thoughts from the consciousness, it will heat up and you can feel it doing so as you hold it. This is indicative of its being charged with electrical thought impulses. If you will transfer it to your left hand, you notice that it will start to cool down. Remember, you are only to program the mineral to clean out those thoughts that are negative, or dormant ones that have not been acted upon. Grudges, fears, grief, and ideas that were not used all fall into the category of the type of thought cleansing (healing) that is desirable.

As the process is occurring in the body, some people notice a bit of dizziness while others experience a feeling of total relaxation. Whatever the reaction, there should be a noticeable difference, even if only in attitude, which is a major help to most of us. Others have reported their crystal turning a bit cloudy. When you feel that your work is finished for each session, take the crystal and, as you hold it, offer it to the universe. Ask the Universal Soul to bring balance to these thoughts and to renew your consciousness so that new and fresh thought beginnings might occur. Perhaps this will help to make each of us more conscious and aware of the importance of acting upon our ideas and plans and releasing our negative emotions. After you have made your offering to the universe, bury the crystal in the ground and do not retrieve it ever again. Because these crystals must be discarded, it is not necessary to use large pieces.

Just to recapitulate, remember that it is of your own choice as to how long you should work with this process during each cleansing session. You can extend it over several minutes or hours in one session, or use several short sessions over a period of several days. Once some semblance of cleanliness and balance is achieved (and only you will know when you have reached that point), you might only feel the need to work in such a manner once a week or less. The choice is yours. After the crystal has been used, bury it in the Earth Mother and leave it there. You will sense a feeling of rebirth and refreshment. It can bring a new beginning.

THE AMETHYST

Besides the use of the pure quartz crystal, Albion gave a session that dealt with the use of the amethyst. This stone was used by the Ancients for various purposes. Research indicates that the amethyst is a form of quartz; its colors being purple, lilac, and sometimes violet. It is found in many places around the world. The deep purple stones have the most monetary value. Some say that the amethyst stone is symbolic of good judgment, justice, and courage. It is known to help keep one sober and also to protect its wearer from black magic. Others believe that the stone is good for different areas of spiritual attunement.

Albion spoke of the amethyst in a different way. "Over and over again, you that live in the material world are confronted with change. These changes occur in every area of your lives. You change friends, residences, jobs, even your personal appearances." He seemed quite intrigued with the people that change their hair coloring or their fashion constantly. "They are trying to create an 'illusion' about themselves. One who does not seek so much physical change is one who is more open and more confident in himself. He is not so filled with fear. It is important to note that each time a change is made, no matter what sort of change it is, major or minor, a new frequency is created. It presents a new energy to be dealt with in the environment and also in your consciousness. Each location on the Earth has its own frequency. Periods of re-adjustment must be gone through after change."

The Teacher also spoke of how we, as people, go through various changes, particularly on the emotional level. Our relationships change. We form relationships of a personal, professional, even spiritual nature, making commitments that we sometimes expect to last forever. Several years down the road, sometimes much less, the commitment ends, the relationship changes. Also, how many times do you encounter people that are going through major periods of growth in their lives due to a specific experience? They change. In short, you change, circumstances change, the planet itself changes. Nothing in the universe remains the same. There is a constant ebb and flow. Life itself is cyclic. The only thing that is absolute is Pure Spirit.

Albion stressed that he had brought these thoughts to our attention so that we would be in the frame of consciousness to realize that change is all around us and that it is natural to life and to the personality. "Change can be positive and it can be negative. It can be a disaster if we resist it. But, it is inevitable."

How many times during any given day do you see

something or someone that makes you say, "I wish I could change that"? Perhaps you wish that you had not responded to another person in a certain manner. Maybe you would like to change a business or personal deal that you have become involved in. Think of how many times we feel this way, not just in a day but over the past ten or twenty-five years, even back into childhood. Time does not stop, and we can't turn back the clock. So often we have to live with the things that, we think or know that we cannot change. But, perhaps this material will serve as an aid to do something about these things in the past and the present, after all.

Albion told us that the Lemurians and the Atlanteans used the amethyst stone for this purpose. They also used it for stability. It is a "change stone". Here is how it will do its work.

First of all, you should choose an amethyst that is as pure as possible and to your liking. In the use of any kind of mineral, you should allow the stone to come to you, paying close attention to the feeling of being drawn to certain ones. Don't choose one that has been polished or made into a piece of jewelry. Let it remain in its natural state. Its size does not matter. It can be one that you purchase or you can also use one that has been given to you. Hold the stone in your hand and designate it with your thoughts as a "change stone". You might say, "You are my Change Stone. I want you to work with me and help me to bring about the changes in my life and consciousness that are desirable to lead me towards a greater sense of progress upon my spiritual path. As I benefit, you will benefit. Your benefit will spread throughout the mineral kingdom." Then, sit in quiet and begin to slowly— we don't want to arouse the emotional body in a negative way by moving too quickly—go back into time in your thoughts. You might want to choose a time in the last month or so that you had a disagreement with someone or a time in the recent past that you may have made an error. Maybe it will simply be some thoughts that you have been holding in your mind that you would like to change. For example: perhaps you have had an argument with your mate or a close friend. The words have left you feeling sad and/or hurt. Hold the amethyst in your hand and remember that incident in your thoughts. Visualize it. You are likely to feel the negative emotions connected with it rise again within yourself. It will most likely be centered in the solar plexus. If you don't feel this, you probably don't have grief or remorse for what occurred and don't feel that you really should or need to change it. You cannot change that which you do not feel a need to change. As the energy begins to rise in the abdomen, create a different scene in your mind. Replay the old scene and then create a new one, one that turns out very differently. You will be mentally constructing a new circumstance. Although it will not change what happened in a physical sense, it will change it in your thoughts. It changes it in your consciousness. And, as we know, thoughts are things. It will telepathically send out the vibrations of this change to the other person involved. The mineral helps to transmit this power. It helps you recreate the scene. This is sending out positive energies to a negative scene that has happened in your life.

Illness needs change and the amethyst can be used to change the physical body, too. Maybe you know someone who is sad or afraid. The stone can then be used for changing these circumstances. You follow the same procedure. If the task is for healing, then visualize the person who is ill as whole and well. If it is for yourself, then hold the stone over the injured or diseased part of your body and ask for change that is right and positive for the condition.

The procedure outlined here is very simple. The amethyst, when not in use, should be stored in a small silk bag or in a box. Don't store it with other stones. Keep it to itself. We are basically talking about the use of positive thinking, along with the mineral, which lends its own force and stability. You can use it in any matter that you feel is necessary for change. All of life is played upon a "cosmic stage". When you recreate the circumstances in your consciousness from negative to positive, you affect all of the universe and the forms within it. The amethyst is a gift from the mineral kingdom to mankind. What a delightful way to use this kingdom for good rather than only a decoration for one's fingers! Let it decorate the consciousness!

CRYSTAL GAZING

BY PAGE BRYANT

The use of a piece of crystal for "seeing" images is a valid and ancient form of psychic work. It is probably one of the most familiar forms of psychic ability with the general public. Some of the resulting images or "visions" can reveal events of the past or the future. This art is known as *scrying*.

It is not difficult to develop the ability to use a crystal ball for purposes of psychic visions and development. I think that it is most important, however, to be properly motivated before beginning such a project. One's psychic energy and ability is not something to experiment with without proper knowledge and preparation.

To prepare your consciousness for any form of psychic or subconscious work, it is a good idea to go through a few minutes of physically relaxing exercises. I suggest sitting down in a straight chair so that your body will be sufficiently supported. Slumping or poor posture can inhibit the results. Start at the feet, silently commanding them to relax. Imagine that the stress and tiredness is flowing out of the soles of the feet, one at a time. You may wish to envision this as a stream of light or color. Move up to the calves of the legs, the upper legs and thighs or hips. Take your time. Also, remember to "see" the stress energy flowing out so that the body can truly relax. As a beginner, never skip this part of your procedure for it is just as important as the psychic work itself and can indeed determine your success. Go on up the entire length of the physical self until you have reached the top of the head. The exercise can be repeated if once is not enough to sufficiently relax you. Once the body is at ease you will have slowed the heart rate and lowered the blood pressure as well. This produces a noticeable and desirable effect, which is the relaxed condition.

The next step is to spread a black or dark-colored cloth on a table in front of you. Choose a table that you can sit at comfortably. Pull your chair close to the table and sit down. Next, place your crystal ball on a stand or flat (most crystal balls have a flattened edge) on the material that covers a portion or all of the table. The dark material serves to reduce the glare coming into the crystal from light in the room. I also suggest that if you do not have a crystal ball, you can substitute a round, glass pie plate. Get one that is pure, clear glass with no writing on it. You may wish to fill it with water after it has been placed on the table and cloth. The water will help add depth to the plate and make it easier to work with.

The next step is to sit with your head slightly

dropped so you can gaze into the crystal or plate on the table. If wayward or distracting thoughts enter your mind, gently push them aside and return to your concentration on the crystal.

You may have to sit several times before you get concrete results. I do not recommend sitting more than fifteen minutes each time, once a day. Whatever time of day you choose to work, it is a good idea to choose the same time each time you work. The subconscious mind is more easily trained by repetition.

You will know you are on the road to success when the crystal begins to "cloud." Once this stage has been reached, images can begin to emerge from the mist . I think it is a good thing to allow the images to be spontaneous at first. As you become more adept with using the crystal you can begin to ask for specific images of the past or the future.

If you should decide to continue using the crystal ball, then you should go about selecting one for purchase. Most crystals are of a fine quality of glass and relatively inexpensive. It is also good to not make a big investment until you are certain of its purpose for you. Real crystal balls are hard to come by and can be very costly. When making your purchase, the clearer the crystal, the better. Watch out for bubbles and glass grains as they can diminish the value of the crystal itself and distract you from your images. Crystals should be selected by yourself personally whenever possible. It is not good to allow any other person to work with your personal crystal. Keep it stored in the black or dark material and in a safe place. Place it safely, where it is not likely to fall, for they can break.

CONCLUSION

The information covered in this book is not scientific but has been channeled through a human consciousness. To properly understand what a true channel is, we must be willing to accept that the higher planes of consciousness can be tapped. Perhaps it involves an alignment of the mind and soul. Man, since his beginnings, has held an affinity for stones. Of this there is no doubt. Modern science and technology has pushed us farther and farther towards a disregard for the value of such methods and procedures. We are more prone to ask how a stone or gem could possibly have an influence on or value for man. The answer may lie purely in the realms of faith. Or, there may be a still greater implicaton involved. We have been moving steadily in the direction of viewing the whole earth as a living, breathing organism. This means that there is an inherent consciousness in all forms of life. The simplicity or complexity of that life makes no difference whatsoever, it is still *life*. What an exciting thought!

As man, we must explore all kingdoms. The task is at-one-ment. Not all vibrations are in harmony with each of us as individuals. This writing is designed to help you, the reader, determine if you are compatible with a few members of the mineral kingdom . . . . crystals. As you journey through this world of substance and matter, perhaps these friends can be of aid. From the minerals we can learn the simplest process of form-building and seek to transfer this knowledge and energy into our own lives . . . . for our own growth and wisdom.

Page Bryant
Flagstaff, Arizona
March 6, 1984

PAGE BRYANT, internationally known psychic, lecturer, and radio personality has expanded her outreach beyond normal dimensions and brings this offering from her spiritual teacher, Albion.

OTHER SUN BOOKS TITLES
you may find of interest:

ASTROLOGY

ALAN LEO'S DICTIONARY OF ASTROLOGY by Alan Leo and Vivian E. Robson. Aaron's Rod, Casting the Horoscope, Disposition, Ecliptic, Equinoxes, Period of Sun, Objects Governed by the Planets, Mean Time.

THE ASTROLOGICAL GUIDE TO HEALTH FOR EACH OF THE TWELVE SUN SIGNS by Ariel Gordon, M.C. Information regarding the twelve signs of the Zodiac is taken from seven of the greatest authorities, past and present, on the different correspondences, as well as from personal experience, extending over many years of private practice.

ASTROLOGY: HOW TO MAKE AND READ YOUR OWN HOROSCOPE by Sepharial. The Alphabet of the Heavens, The Construction of a Horoscope, How to Read the Horoscope, The Stars in Their Courses.

A BEGINNER'S GUIDE TO PRACTICAL ASTROLOGY by Vivian E. Robson. How to Cast a Horoscope, Planets, Signs, and Houses, How to Judge a Horoscope, How to Calculate Future Influences, etc.

THE BOWL OF HEAVEN by Evangeline Adams. My Job and How I Do It, A Grim Success, A Tale of Two Cities, "Dabbling in Heathenism", A Horrible Example, We are All Children of the Stars, Life and Death, The Money-Makers, Some Ladies of Venus, I Never Gamble, A World in Love, Astrological Marriages, My Own and Others, The New Natology, Twins and Things, Why Most People Come to Me, Am I Always Right? As I See It.

THE COSMIC KEY OF LIFE SELF-REALIZATION by A.S. Vickers. Index Charts, The Cosmic Key of Life, Helps in Selecting a Goal, Concentration, What is a Science? Key to Horoscope Blanks, Horoscopes of Noted Persons, Planetary Positions, Planetary Aspects, Sign Keywords, Appendix To Students, Astrological Smiles, Index to Astrological Attributes.

THE DIVINE LANGUAGE OF CELESTIAL CORRESPONDENCES by Coulson Turnbull. Esoteric Symbolism of the Planets, Mystical Interpretation of the Zodiac, Kabalistical Interpretation of the 12 Houses, Evolution and Involution of Soul, Character of the Planets, Hermetic Books, Nature of Signs, Etc.

THE EARTH IN THE HEAVENS - RULING DEGREES OF CITIES - HOW TO FIND AND USE THEM by L. Edward Johndro. Precession, Midheavens and Ascendants, Calculating Midheavens and Ascendants, Use of Locality Angles, Verification by World Events, Applications to Nativities.

1

ECLIPSES IN THEORY AND PRACTICE by Sepharial. The Natural Cause of an Eclipse, Eclipses of the Sun, Lunar Eclipses, Historical Eclipses, To Calculate an Eclipse of the Sun, To Calculate a Lunar Eclipse, Eclipse Signs, Eclipse Indications, The Decanates, Transits over Eclipse Points, Individuals and Eclipses, Illustrations, Conclusion.

HEBREW ASTROLOGY by Sepharial. Chaldean Astronomy, Time and Its Measures, The Great Year, The Signs of the Zodiac, How to Set a Horoscope, The Seven Times, Modern Predictions.

THE INFLUENCE OF THE ZODIAC UPON HUMAN LIFE by Eleanor Kirk. The Quickening Spirit, Questions and Answers, Disease, Development, A Warning, Marriage, The Fire, Air, Earth, and Water Triplicities, Etc. (This is an excellent book!)

THE LIGHT OF EGYPT or THE SCIENCE OF THE SOUL AND THE STARS by Thomas H. Burgoyne. Vol. 1: Realms of Spirit and Matter, Mysteries of Sex, Incarnation and Re-Incarnation, Karma, Mediumship, Soul Knowledge, Mortality and Immortality. Basic Principles of Celestial Science, Stellar Influence on Humanity, Alchemical Nature of Man, Union of Soul and Stars. Vol. II: The Zodiac and the Constellations, Spiritual Interpretation of the Zodiac, Astro-Theology and Astro-Mythology, Symbolism and Alchemy, Talismans and Ceremonial Magic, Tablets of AEth including: The Twelve Mansions, The Ten Planetary Rulers, The Ten Great Powers of the Universe, and Penetralia – The Secret of the Soul.

MANUAL OF ASTROLOGY by Sepharial. Language of the Heavens, Divisions of the Zodiac, Planets, Houses, Aspects, Calculation of the Horoscope, Reading of a Horoscope, Measure of Time, Law of Sex, Hindu Astrology, Progressive Horoscope, Etc.

MEDICAL ASTROLOGY by Henrich Däath. Basic Elements, Anatomical Sign-Rulership, Planetary Powers and Principles,Biodynamic Actions of Planets,How the Planets Crystallise in Organic and Inorganic Life, Tonicity, Atonicity and Perversion, Zodiaco-Planetary Synopsis of Typical Diseases, The Sixth and Eight Houses, The Triplicities and Quadruplicities, Planetary Sympathy and Antipathy, Guaging Planetary Strengths in the Specific Horoscope, Application, Examples, Indications of Short Life

NEW DICTIONARY OF ASTROLOGY IN WHICH ALL TECHNICAL AND ABSTRUSE TERMS USED IN THE TEXT BOOKS OF THE SCIENCE ARE INTIMATELY EXPLAINED AND ILLUSTRATED By Sepharial Everything from Abscission to Zuriel.

THE PLANETS THROUGH THE SIGNS: Astrology for Living, by Abbe Bassett. Includes chapters on the Sun, Moon, and various planets, and how each one influences us through the different signs of the Zodiac.

PRIMARY DIRECTIONS MADE EASY by Sepharial. Principles of Directing, Polar Elevations, Illustrations, Mundane Aspects, Zodiacal Parallels, Mundane Parallels, Summary, Further Examples, Suggested Method, General Review, The Royal Horoscope, The Telescopic View, Solar and Lunar Horoscopes, Appendix.

RAPHAEL'S GUIDE TO ASTROLOGY by Raphael. The Symbols Explained, The Nature of the Aspects and Signs, The Orbits of the Planets, Persons Produced by the Signs of The Zodiac, The Form of Body Given by the Planets in the Signs, The Use of an Ephemeris, How to Erect a Map of the Heavens, How to Place the Planets in the Map, The Nature of the Planets, How to Judge a Nativity, Whether a Child Will Live or Die, Health, Mental Qualities, Money, Employment, Marriage, Travel, Etc., On the Selection of a House, Friends and Enemies, Directions or Calculating Future Events, A Short Astrological Dictionary, Etc!

RAPHAEL'S KEY TO ASTROLOGY by Raphael. Planetary Aspects and Orbs, Description of Persons Produced by the Signs, The Use of an Ephemeris, How to Erect a Map of the Heavens, The Influence of the Planets, How to Judge a Nativity, Whether a Child Will Live or Die, Health and Mental Qualities, Money Prospects and Employment, Marriage, Children and Travel, Friends and Enemies, The Kind of Death, etc.

RAPHAEL'S MEDICAL ASTROLOGY or the Effects of the Planets on the Human Body by Raphael. The Zodiac and the Human Body, Planetary Rulership and Action, Health and Constitution, Physical Condition, The Duration of Life, Examples of Early Death, Diseases, Mental Disorders, Injuries, Accidents and Deformities, Health and the Horoscope, Preventive Measures, Herbal Remedies, the Course of Disease, Astrology and Colors, etc.

RAPHAEL'S MUNDANE ASTROLOGY OR THE EFFECTS OF THE PLANETS AND SIGNS UPON THE NATIONS AND COUNTRIES OF THE WORLD by Raphael. Mundane Astrology, Planetary and Zodiacal Signs and Symbols, The Twelve Mundane Houses, The Significations of the Planets, Essential and Accidental Dignities, The Mundane Map, Concerning the Houses and the Planets, How to Judge a Mundane Map, Ellipses, Earthquakes, Comets, Planetary Conjunctions, The Parts of the World Affected by the Signs of the Zodiac. etc.

RELATION OF THE MINERAL SALTS OF THE BODY TO THE SIGNS OF THE ZODIAC by Dr. George W. Carey. Biochemistry, Esoteric Chemistry, The Ultimate of Biochemistry, The Twelve Cell-Salts of the Zodiac, Aries: The Lamb of God, Taurus: The Winged Bull, The Chemistry of Gemini, Cancer: The Chemistry of the Crab, Leo: The Heart of the Zodiac, Virgo: The Virgin Mary, Libra: The Loins, Scorpio: Influence of the Blood, The Chemistry of Sagittarius, Capricorn: The Goat of the Zodiac, The Sign of the Son of Man: Aquarius, Pisces: The Fish That Swim in the Pure Sea.

THE RISING ZODIACAL SIGN: ITS MEANING AND PROGNOSTICS by Coulson Turnbull. Aries - The Ram, Taurus - The Bull, Gemini - The Twins, Cancer - The Crab, Leo - The Lion, Virgo - The Virgin, Libra - The Balance, Scorpio - The Scorpion, Sagittarius - The Arrow, Capricorn - The Goat, Aquarius - The Waterman, Pisces - The Fishes, How To Determine the Rising Sign, Tables I, II, and III.

THE SCIENCE OF FOREKNOWLEDGE AND THE RADIX SYSTEM by Sepharial. The Science of Foreknowledge, Astrology in Shakespeare, The Great Year, Celestial Dynamics, Neptune, The Astrology of Lilith, Indian Astrology, Horoscope of Rama, Astrology of The Hebrews, Joan of Arc, The Measure of Life, Astrological Practice, Methods of Ptolemy and Benatti, The Radix System, Horoscopical Anomalies, Our Solar System, Financial Astrology.

THE SILVER KEY: A GUIDE TO SPECULATIORS by Sepharial. The Furure Method, Science of Numbers, Finding the Winner, The Lunar Key, Gravity and Evolution, Something to Come, A Warning, On Specilation, Monte Carlo and Astrology, Tables of Sidereal Times, Tables of Ascendants, Etc!

THE SOLAR EPOCH A NEW ASTROLOGICAL THESIS by Sepharial. The History of Birth, The Lunar Horoscope, The Solar Horoscope, Directional Influences, Conclusions.

THE SOLAR LOGOS OR STUDIES IN ARCANE MYSTICISM BY Coulson Turnbull. The Logos, The Kingdom of the Soul, Intuition and Motion, The Mystic Macrocosm, The Spirit of the Planets, The Mystical Sun and Moon, The Soul in Action, The Spiritual Horoscope, Health, Disease, Service, Etc.

THE STARS - HOW AND WHERE THEY INFLUENCE by L. Edward Johndro. Theory, Astronomical Fundamentals, Application of Fixed Stars to Nativities, Application of fixed Stars to Mundane Astrology, Verification by Nativities, Verification by World Events, Variable Stars, Binary Stars, Double Stars, Clusters, Nebulae and Bright Stars, General and Technical, Considerations, Conclusion.

STARS OF DESTINY – THE ANCIENT SCIENCE OF ASTROLOGY AND HOW TO MAKE USE OF IT TODAY by Katherine Taylor Craig. History and description of the Science, The Sun From Two Standpoints, The Moon and the Planets. Astrological Predictions That Have Been Verified, Practical Directions for Casting a Horoscope, Sample of General Prediction for a Year.

A STUDENTS' TEXT-BOOK OF ASTROLOGY by Vivian E. Robson. Fundamental Principles of Astrology, Casting the Horoscope, Character and Mind, Occupation and Position, Parents, Relatives and Home, Love and Marriage, Esoteric Astrology, Adoption of the New Style Calendar.

WHAT IS ASTROLOGY? by Colin Bennett. How an Astrologer Works, Sign Meanings, How Aspects Affect a Horoscope, Numerology as an Astrological Aid, Psychology In Relation to Astrology, Etc.

ATLANTIS / LEMURIA

ATLANTIS IN AMERICA by Lewis Spence. Atlantis and Antillia, Cro-Magnons of America. Quetzalcoatl the Atlantean, Atlantis in American Tradition and Religion, Ethnological Evidence, Art and Architecture, Folk-Memories of an Atlantic Continent, Analogy of Lemuria, Chronological Table, Etc.

THE PROBLEM OF LEMURIA - THE SUNKEN CONTINENT OF THE PACIFIC by Lewis Spence, Illustrated. The Legend of Lemuria, The Argument From Archaeology, The Testimony of Tradition, The Evidence from Myth and Magic, The Races of Lemuria, The Testimony of Custom, The Proof of Art, The Geology of Lemuria, The Evidence from Biology, The Catastrophe and its Results, Life and Civilization in Lemuria, Atlantis and Lemuria, Conclusions.

WISDOM FROM ATLANTIS by Ruth B. Drown. Being, Divine Selfishness, Service, Nobility of Self-Reliance, Harmony, Divine Love, Principles of Life and Living, Man's Divine Nature, Faith, True Thinking.

AUTOSUGGESTION / HYPNOTISM

SELF MASTERY THROUGH CONSCIOUS AUTOSUGGESTION by Emile Coué. Self Mastery Through Autosuggestion, Thoughts and Precepts, What Autosuggestion Can Do, Education as it Ought to Be, A Survey of the "Seances", the Miracle Within, Everything for Everyone, Etc.

THE PRACTICE OF AUTOSUGGESTION BY THE METHOD OF EMILE COUÉ by C. Harry Brooks. The Clinic of Emile Coué, A Few of Coué's Cures, Thought is a Force, Thought and the Will, The General Formula, How to Deal With Pain, Autosuggestion and the Child, Particular Suggestions, Etc.

MY METHOD by Emile Coué. Chapters Include: Autosuggestion Disconcerting in its Simplicity, Slaves of Suggestion and Masters of Ourselves, Dominance of the Imagination over the Will, The Moral Factor in all Disease, Don't Concentrate, How to Banish Pain, Psychic Culture as Necessary as Physical, Self-Mastery Means Health, Etc.

HOW TO PRACTICE SUGGESTION AND AUTOSUGGESTION by Emile Coué, Preface by Charles Baudouin. Interviews of Patients, Examples of the Power of Suggestion and Autosuggestion, Suggestions: General and Special, Special Suggestions for Each Ailment, Advice to Patients, Lectures Delivered by Emile Coué in America.

EMILE COUÉ: THE MAN AND HIS WORK by Hugh MacNaughten Foreword and Author's Notes, Prelude, Nancy, Nancy or London, M Coué at Eton, M Coué in London, The Sub-Concious Self, On Some Stumbling Blocks, M Coué in His Relation To Christianity, On "Everything for Nothing", M. Coué, Envoi

CHRISTIANITY AND AUTOSUGGESTION by C. Harry Brooks and Rev. Ernest Charles. Autosuggestion and the Teachings of Christ, Christ the Healer, What is Faith? Faith and Autosuggestion, Christ and the Will, The Power Within, Alliance of Christianity and Autosuggestion, God and the Unconscious, The Christian Formula, Christian Specific Suggestion, Temptation, The Child, Pain, Some Objections (Including Opposition of Organized Christianity to New Discoveries).

AUTO-SUGGESTION:WHAT IT IS AND HOW TO USE IT FOR HEALTH, HAPPINESS AND SUCCESS by Herbert A. Parkvn. M.D.. C.M. Auto-suggestion - What it is and how to use it, Auto-suggestion - Its effects and how to employ it to overcome physical troubles, Auto-suggestion - How to employ it to overcome mental troubles, Influences of early auto-suggestions for the forming of the character, Auto-suggestion for the formation of habits, Auto-suggestion and personal magnetism, The cultivation of optimism through auto-suggestion, Auto-suggestion for developing concentration, The achievement of success through auto-suggestion and success, Auto-suggestion and breathing exercises, Auto-suggestion: It's influence on health in the winter, The diagnosis and treatment of a typical case of chronic physical suffering, Auto-suggestion the basis of all healing, How psychic pictures are made realities by auto-suggestion.

CLAIRVOYANCE

SECOND SIGHT - A STUDY OF NATURAL AND INDUCED CLAIRVOYANCE by Sepharial. The Scientific Position, Materials and Conditions, The Faculty of Seership, Preliminaries and Practice, Kinds of Visions, Obstacles and Clairvoyance, Symbolism, Allied Psychic Phases, Experience and Use.

CONSPIRACY

THE ILLUMINOIDS – SECRET SOCIETIES AND POLITICAL PARANOIA by Neal Wilgus. Detailed picture of Weishaupt's Order of the Illuminati as well as other secret societies throughout history. Ties various far-reaching areas together including important information relating to the J.F. Kennedy assassination. "The best single reference on the Illuminati in fact and legendry" – Robert Anton Wilson in Cosmic Trigger.

CRYSTALS/MINERALS

CRYSTALS AND THEIR USE—A Study of At-One-Ment with the Mineral Kingdom by Page Bryant. Mineral Consciousness, Crystals and Their Use, Sacred Centers, Various Types of Crystals, The Amethyst, Crystal Gazing.

THE MAGIC OF MINERALS by Page Bryant. The Inner Lives of the Mineral Kingdom, Megalithic Mysteries and the Native American View, The Healing Properties of Minerals, Psychic Influences in Minerals, Stones of the Zodiac, Crystals and Their Use, General Information on Selection, Use, and Care of Minerals.

MAN, MINERALS, AND MASTERS by Charles W. Littlefield, M.D. School of the Magi, Three Masters, The Cubes, Initiation in Tibet, Hindustan, and Egypt, History, Prophecy, Numerology, Perfection. 172p. 5x8 Paperback.

PLANETARY INFLUENCES AND THERAPEUTIC USES OF PRECIOUS STONES by George Frederick Kunz. Includes various lists and illustrations, etc.

DREAMS

DREAMS AND PREMONITIONS by L.W. Rogers. Introduction, The Dreamer, The Materialistic Hypotheses Inadequate, Dreams of Discovery, Varieties of Dreams, Memories of Astral Experiences, Help from the Invisibles, Premonitory Dreams, Dreams of the Dead, How to Remember Dreams.

EARTH CHANGES (Also See Prophecy)

CHEIRO'S WORLD PREDICTIONS by Cheiro. Fate of Nations, British Empire in its World Aspect, Destiny of the United States, Future of the Jews, Coming War of Wars, Coming Aquarian Age, Precession of the Equinoxes.

THE COMING STAR-SHIFT AND MANY PROPHECIES OF BIBLE AND PYRAMID FULFILLED by O. Gordon Pickett. God Corrects His Clock in the Stars, English Alphabet as Related to Numerics, Joseph Builder of the Great Pyramid, Numerical Harmony, Prophecy, World Wars, Star-Shifts, The Flood, Astronomy, The Great Pyramids, Etc.

COMING WORLD CHANGES by H.A. and F.H.Curtiss. The Prophecies, Geological Considerations, The Philosophy of Planetary Changes, The King of the World, The Heart of the World, The Battle of Armageddon, The Remedy.

EARTH CHANGES NOW! by Page Bryant. The Earth is Changing: The Evidence, We Knew it was Coming!, The Sacred Covenant, The Externalization of the Spiritual Hierarchy, The Earth Angel: A Promise for the Future.

THE EARTH CHANGES SURVIVAL HANDBOOK by Page Bryant. The Emergence of Planetary Intelligence, Mapping the Earth, Earth Changes: Past and Future,

Preparing for the Future, Walking in Balance, Etc.

NOSTRADAMUS NOW - PROPHECIES OF PERIL AND PROMISE FOR THE 1990'S AND BEYOND by Joseph Robert Jochmans Chapters include: What Were the Prophet's Secret Sources of Wisdom? What Mysterious Methods Did the Prophet Use to Make His Forecasts? Will the Prophet Return to Life? A Warning of Coming Global War For Our World Today? Is America About to Suffer Social, Political and Economic Collapse? Will Superquakes Devastate America's West and East Coasts? Is a Planetary Inter-Dimensional Doorway About to Be Opened? The Middle East Gulf War Was It Necessary, and Will It Flare Up Again? The Coming of the Man of Power From the East: Antichrist or Avatar? When Will the Downfall of the World Economic System Take Place? Could a Comet or Meteor Hit the Earth and Cause an Axis Pole Shift? Where Will be the Trouble Spots in the Middle East and Far East During the Next Ten Years? What Major Earth Cataclysms May Yet Occur? The New Russia and America Have They Changed For the Better? What Will Be Humanity's Destiny Into the Far Future? Which Future Options Will We Choose?

ORACLES OF NOSTRADAMUS by Charles A. Ward. Life of Nostradamus, Preface to Prophecies, Epistle to Henry II, Magic, Historic Fragments, Etc.

PROPHECIES OF GREAT WORLD CHANGES compiled by George B. Brownell. World-War Prophecies, Coming Changes of Great Magnitude, False Christs, The New Heaven and the New Earth, The New Order and the Old, Etc.

ROLLING THUNDER: THE COMING EARTH CHANGES by J. R. Jochmans. The Coming Famine and Earth Movements, The Destruction of California and New York, Future War, Nostradamus, Bible, Edgar Cayce, Coming Avatars, Pyramid Prophecy, Weather, Coming False Religion and the Antichrist, and much, much more! This book is currently our best selling title.

UTOPIA II: AN INVESTIGATION INTO THE KINGDOM OF GOD by John Schmidt. Why Utopia?, Mankind's Past, Present, and Future, A Sociological Look, A Political Look, An Economic Look, A Spiritual Look.

GENERAL OCCULT

ANCIENT MYSTERY AND MODERN REVELATION by W.J. Colville. Rivers of Life or Faiths of Man in All Lands, Ancient and Modern Ideas of Revelation - Its Sources and Agencies, Creation Legends - How Ancient is Humanity On this Planet? Egypt and Its Wonders: Literally and Mystically Considered, The Philosophy of Ancient Greece, The School of Pythagoras, The Delphic Mysteries, Apollonius of Tyana, Five Varieties of Yoga, Union of Eastern and Western Philosophy, Ezekial's Wheel - What it Signifies, The Book of Exodus - Its Practical and Esoteric Teachings, The Message of Buddhism - Purity and Philanthropy, Magic in Europe in the Middle Ages, Ancient Magic and Modern Therapeutics, Bible Symbolism, The Law of Seven and the Law of Unity, The Esoteric Teachings of the Gnostics.

BYGONE BELIEFS – AN EXCURSION INTO THE OCCULT AND ALCHEMICAL NATURE OF MAN by H. Stanley Redgrove. Some Characteristics of Mediaeval Thought, Pythagoras and his Philosophy, Medicine and Magic, Belief in Talismans, Ceremonial Magic in Theory and Practice, Architectural Symbolism, Philosopher's Stone, The Phallic Element in Alchemical Doctrine, Roger Bacon, Etc. (Many Illustrations).

THE BOOK OF CHARMS AND TALISMANS by Sepharial. History and Background, Numbers and their Significance, Charms to Wear, Background of Talismans, Making Talismans.

THE COILED SERPENT by C.J. van Vliet. A Philosophy of Conservation and Transmutation of Reproductive Energy. Deadlock in Human Evolution, Spirit Versus Matter, Sex Principle and Purpose of Sex, Pleasure Principle, Unfolding of Spirit, Marriage and Soul-Mates, Love Versus Sex, Erotic Dreams, Perversion and Normalcy, Virility, Health, and Disease, Freemasonry, Rosicrucians, Alchemy, Astrology, Theosophy, Magic, Yoga, Occultism, Path of Perfection, Uncoiling the Serpent, The Future, Supermen, Immortality, Etc.

COSMIC SYMBOLISM by Sepharial. Meaning and Purpose of Occultism, Cosmic Symbology, Reading the Symbols, Law of Cycles, Time Factor in Kabalism, Involution and Evolution, Planetary Numbers, Sounds, Hours, Celestial Magnetic Polarities, Law of Vibrations, Lunar and Solar Influences, Astrology and the Law of Sex, Character and Environment, Etc.

A DICTIONARY OF NON-CLASSICAL MYTHOLOGY by Marian Edwardes & Lewis Spence An exceptional work! "Not one mythology, but several, will be found concentrated within the pages of this volume . . ." Covers everything from Aah (Ah): An Egyptian moon-god, thru Brigit: A goddess of the Irish Celts, Excalibur: King Arthur's Sword, Hou Chi: A Chinese divine personage, . . . Huitzilopochtli of the Aztecs . . . Mama Cocha of Peru . . . Uttu: The Sumerian . . . Valkyrie (Old German): Female warriors . . . Byelun: A white Russian deity, . . . Meke Meke: The god-creator of Easter Island, Mwari: The Great Spirit of the Mtawara tribe of Rhodesia, Triglav (Three heads): Baltic Slav deity, and hundreds more!

INFINITE POSSIBILITIES by Leilah Wendell. Chapters include: The Essence of Time, Time and Space, Inseperable Brothers, Coexistent Time, Traveling Through Time, Microcosmic Reflections, Cosmic Consciousness, The Universe in a Jar, Psychic Alchemy, Universality, The Divine Element, The Complete Whole, What Price Immortality?, Practical Infinity, Etc.

THE INNER GOVERNMENT OF THE WORLD by Annie Besant. Ishvara, The Builders of a Cosmos, The Hierarchy of our World, The Rulers, Teachers, Forces, Method of Evolution, Races and Sub-Races, The Divine Plan, Religions and Civilizations, Etc.

THE MASCULINE CROSS AND ANCIENT SEX WORSHIP by Sha Rocco. Origin of the Cross, Emblems: Phallus, Triad, Vocabulary, Marks and Signs of the Triad, Yoni, Color of Gods, Fish and Good Friday, Tortoise, Earth Mother, Unity, Fourfold God, Meru, Religious Prostitution, Shaga, Communion Buns and Religious Cakes, Antiquity of the Cross, Crucifixion, Christna, Phallic and Sun Worship, The Phallus in California.

THE OCCULT ARTS by J.W. Frings. Alchemy, Astrology, Psychometry, Telepathy, Clairvoyance, Spiritualism, Hypnotism, Geomancy, Palmistry, Omens and Oracles.

THE OCCULT ARTS OF ANCIENT EGYPT by Bernard Bromage. Foreword, The Nature of the Ancient Egyptian Civilization, What the Ancient Egyptians Understood by Magic, The Destiny of the Soul According to the Egyptians, Egyptian Magic and Belief in Amulets and Talismans, The Egyptian Magicians, Black Magic in Ancient Egypt, The Astrological Implications of Egyptian Magic, Ancient Egypt and the Universal Dream Life, (Includes Various Illustrations).

OCCULTISTS & MYSTICS OF ALL AGES by Ralph Shirley. Apollonius of Tyana, Plotinus, Michael Scot, Paracelsus, Emanuel Swedenborg, Count Cagliostro, Anna Kingsford.

SEMA-KANDA: THRESHOLD MEMORIES by Coulson Turnbull. Ra-Om-Ar and Sema-Kanda, The Brotherhood, Sema-Kanda's Childhood, The Scroll, Posidona, Questioning, Ramantha's Lesson, The Great White Lodge, The Destruction of Atlantis, The Two Prisoners, The Congregation of the Inquisition, An Invitation, A Musical Evening, Two Letters, Confidences, The Horoscope, Etc.

VOICE OF ISIS by H.A. & F.A. Curtiss. Life's Duties, The Cycle of Fulfillment, Degrees and Orders, The Wisdom Religion, Concerning the Doctrine of Hell Fire, The Eleventh Commandment, Narcotics, Alcohol and Phychism, A Study of Karma, The Self, The Doctrine of Avatara, The Study of Reincarnation, Power, A Brief Outline of Evolution, The Laws, World Chains, Purity, The Origin of Man, The Symbol of the Serpent, Purification vs Deification, The Memory of Past Lives, The Cycle of Necessity, Etc!

YOUR UNSEEN GUIDE by C.J. Halsted. The Manner in Which You are Guided, How I Am Guided Consciously, Omens, The Intermediate State, Heaven, Spiritualism, The "Spirit Man" Illusion Dispelled, Evidence of My Guide's Prescience, Evolution.

WHAT IS OCCULTISM? by Papus. Occultism Defined, Occult Philosophical Point of View, Ethics of Occultism, Aesthetics of Occultism, Theodicy – Sociology, Practice of Occultism, The Traditions of Magic, Occultism and Philosophy.

GRAPHOLOGY

HOW TO READ CHARACTER IN HANDWRITING by Mary H. Booth. Principles of Analysis and Deduction, Forming Impressions from the Handwriting, The Autograph Fad, Entertaining by Graphology, Graphology as a Profession, Index.

HEALING

CHINESE SYSTEM OF HEALING by Denis Lawson-Wood, L.Th., Ph.D. Theoretical Basis and Practical Treatment, Standard Terms and Symbols, On the Meridians and Points, Numerical List of Points, Diagrams, Alphabetical Index of Chinese Names, Alphabetical Index of English Names , Alphabetical Index of Homeopathic Remedies, Alphabetical Index of Bach Herbal Remedies, Psychological Conditions, Physical Symptoms, Appendix.

DIVINE REMEDIES – A TEXTBOOK ON CHRISTIAN HEALING by Theodosia DeWitt Schobert. Fuller Understanding of Spiritual Healing, Healing of Blood Troubles and Skin Diseases, Freedom from Sense Appetite, Healing of Insanity, Healing of Insomnia, Healing of Poisoning of Any Kind, General Upbuilding and Healing of the Body Temple.

THE FINER FORCES OF NATURE IN DIAGNOSIS AND THERAPY by George Starr White, M.D. The Magnetic Meridian, Vital and Unseen Forces, Polarity, Cause of Un-Health, Colors, Magnetic Energy, Sympathetic-Vagal Reflex, Actions of Finer Forces of Nature, The Human Aura, Moon-Light and Sound Treatment with Light and Color, Etc.

HEAL THYSELF: AN EXPLANATION OF THE REAL CAUSE AND CURE OF DISEASE by Edward Bach, M.B., B.S., D.P.H. by focusing on the causes rather than the results of disease and thus allowing individuals to assist in their own healing, Dr. Bach shows the vital principles which will guide medicine in the near future and are indeed guiding some of the more advanced members of the profession today.

HEALTH AND SPIRITUAL HEALING by Richard Lynch. The Key to Health, Statements for the Realization of Health, Rhythm of Life and Health, The Revelation of the Body, Realizing the Perfect Body, The Tree of Life and Health, Establishing the Incorruptible Body, Health Personified, Bringing Forth the True Body, How to Renew Your Consciousness, Individual Rebirth in Consciousness, Individual Resurrection, Ideas for Individual Ressurrection.

THE KEY TO MAGNETIC HEALING by J.H. Strasser. The History of Magnetic Healing, The Theory of Magnetic Healing, Proof of Its Existence, What it is, Sources of it, Are Vital Magnetism and Electricity the Same, Have all Persons Magnetic Power?, Mental Science, The Principle of Life in Man, Mind and Magnetism, The Will Power, Mind over Matter, Passivity or Hypnotism, Why is Suggestion so Effective during Passivity?, Telepathy, Experiments, Testing Susceptibility, To Find Hidden Objects, Producing the Passive State, Suggestion, Manipulation, and Passes, General Treatment by Suggestion, Producing Anaesthesia, Hypnotizing at a Distance, Suggestion during Common Sleep, Suggestion during Waking State, Telepathy or Mind—Telegraphy, The Practice of Magnetic Healing, Can Magnetic Healing be Suppressed?, Unconscious Magnetic Healing, Treatment of the Different Diseases, Nervous Diseases, Blood Diseases, caused by Congestion and Irregular Circulation, Miscellaneous Diseases, Etc!

THE PHILOSOPHY OF MENTAL HEALING – A PRACTICAL EXPOSITION OF NATURAL RESTORATIVE POWER by Leander Edmund Whipple. Metaphysical Healing, Metaphysics Versus Hypnotism, The Potency of Metaphysics in Surgery, The Progress of the Age, Intelligence and Sensation, Mental Action, The Physical Reflection of Thought.

THE PRINCIPLES OF OCCULT HEALING Edited by Mary Weeks Burnett, M.D. Occult Healing and Occultism, Healing and the Healing Intelligence. The Indestructible Self, Latent Powers of Matter, The Auras and the Ethers, Polarization, Music, Healing by Prayer, Angel or Deva Helpers, Thought Forms and Color in Healing, Magnetism – Mesmerism, Healing Miracles of the Christ, Etc

THE TWELVE HEALERS AND OTHER REMEDIES by Edward Bach. Chapters include remedies for the following: For Fear, For Uncertainty, For Insufficient Interest in Present Circumstances, For Loneliness, For Those Over-Sensitive to Influences and Ideas, For Despondency or Despair, For Over-Care for Welfare of Others.

HERBS

THE COMPLETE HERBALIST or THE PEOPLE THEIR OWN PHYSICIANS by Dr. O. Phelps Brown. By the use of Nature's Remedies great curative properties found in the Herbal Kingdom are described. A New and Plain System of Hygienic Principles Together with Comprehensive Essays on Sexual Philosophy, Marriage, Divorce, Etc.

THE TRUTH ABOUT HERBS by Mrs. C.F. Loyd. The Unbroken Tradition of Herbal Medicine, The History of Herbalism, The Birth of the Society of Herbalists, Herbs Cure-The Reason Why, The Healing Properties of Certain Herbs, The Effect of Herbs on Allergic Diseases, Herbalists' Fight for Freedom, Etc.

HISTORICAL NOVEL

CHILD OF THE SUN by Frank Cheavens. Alvar Nuñez Cabeza de Vaca was the first European explorer to cross the North American continent. His early 16th century wandering took him across Texas, part of New Mexico, southeastern Arizona, and down the west coast of Mexico into South America. His altruistic work and healing ministrations among the Indians of the Southwest drew to him multitudes of Indians who revered him as the Child of the Sun. Here, his story is told through the eyes of a deformed, itinerant Pueblo trader who joined him, studied with him, and witnessed the Great Spirit working through him.

HOLLOW EARTH

ETIDORHPA or THE END OF EARTH by John Uri Lloyd. Journey toward the center of the Earth thru mighty mushroom forests and across huge underground oceans with an entire series of fantastic experiences. A true occult classic! "Etidorhpa, the End of Earth, is in all respects the worthiest presentation of occult teachings under the attractive guise of fiction that has yet been written" – New York World.

INSPIRATION / POSITIVE THINKING / SELF HELP

CREATIVE MIND by Ernest S. Holmes. Chapters include: In the Beginning, Why and What is a Man?, The Law of Our Lives, Bondage and Freedom, The Word, The Power We Have Within Us, The Reason for the Universe, Mind in Action, Action and Reaction, Arriving at High Consciousness, The Perfect Universe, About Struggle Karma, Etc.

CRISIS IN CONSCIOUSNESS: The Source of All Conflict by Robert Powell. The Importance of Right Beginning, Zen and Liberation, The Worldly Mind and the Religious Mind, Repetition of the Pattern, Experience, Habit and Freedom, Can Illumination be Transmitted? The Equation of Unhappiness, Must We Have Religious Societies? Approach to the Immeasurable, Window on Non-Duality, Memory Without a Cause, Self or Non-Self? Common Sayings Revealing Uncommon Insights, On Contradiction, The Outer and the Inner, Etc.

THE FAITH THAT HEALS (HOW TO DEVELOP) by Fenwicke L. Holmes The New Consciousness, Cosmic Consciousness, The Law of Consciousness Outlines, Practical Use of Visions – Visualizing Prosperity and Health, the Cure of Organic Disease and "Incurables," New Healing and Prosperity Consciousness, Your Healing Word, Faith in Yourself, Developing Self-Confidence, etc.

THE FREE MIND: THE INWARD PATH TO LIBERATION by Robert Powell. Liberation and Duality, Crisis in Consciousness, Our Predicament, On Mindfulness, Living in the Essential, A Noncomparative Look at Zen and Krishnamurti, The Problem of Ambition, Only the Empty Mind is Capable of True Thoughtfulness, What Education Should Be All About, and What it Actually Is, If Awareness is Choiceless, Then Who is it That is Aware?, Free Among the Unfree, The Vicious, Vicious Circle of Self-Defense and War, Reflections on Causality: The Ultimate Failure of Metaphysics, Etc.

HEALTH AND WEALTH FROM WITHIN by William E. Towne. Health From Within, Awakening of the Soul, Will, Love and Work, The Voice of Life, Non-Attachment, The Woman – The Man, The Supreme Truth, Power of Imagination and Faith, Practical Self-Healing, The Way to Gain Results, Lengthen and Brighten Life, Etc.

INNER RADIANCE by H.A. & F.A. Curtiss. The Inner Radiance, Spiritual Co-operation, Man and the Zodiac, The Soul-Language, Transmigration, Cosmic Cause of World Conditions, Planetary and Karmic Factors, The Mystic Rose, The Lords of Karma, The Great Works, The Mystery of the Elements, The Third Eye, The Round Table, The Ancient Continents, Nature's Symbology.

SO SPEAKS HIGHER POWER: A HANDBOOK FOR EMOTIONAL AND SPIRITUAL RECOVERY by Dr. Isaac Shamaya. Addiction, Stress and Recovery, Feeling, Blame, Anger, Fear and Pain, Relationships, Understanding, Love, and Higher Power.

THE SUCCESS PROCESS by Brown Landone. Five Factors Which Guarantee Success. The Process of Vivid Thinking, Tones Used in Persuading, Use of Action, Overcoming Hindrances, Developing Capacities, Securing Justice, Augmenting Your Success by Leadership, Etc.

THOUGHT FORCES by Prentice Mulford. Chapters include: Co-operation of Thought, Some Practical Mental Recipes, The Drawing Power of Mind, Buried Talents, The Necessity of Riches, The Uses of Sickness, The Doctor Within, Mental Medicine, The Use and Necessity of Recreation, The Art of Forgetting, Cultivate Repose, Love Thyself.

VISUALIZATION AND CONCENTRATION AND HOW TO CHOOSE A CAREER by Fenwicke L. Holmes. The Creative Power of Mind, Metaphysics and Psychology, Mental Telepathy, Visualization and Dramatization, Concentration How to Choose a Career.

JAMES ALLEN TITLES

ABOVE LIFE'S TURMOIL by James Allen. True Happiness, The Immortal Man, The Overcoming of Self, The Uses of Temptation, The Man of Integrity, Discrimination, Belief, The Basis of Action, The Belief that Saves, Thought and Action, Your Mental Attitude, Sowing and Reaping, The Reign of Law, The Supreme Justice, The Use of Reason, Self-Discipline, Resolution, The Glorious Conquest, Contentment in Activity, The Temple of Brotherhood, Pleasant Pastures of Peace.

ALL THESE THINGS ADDED by James Allen. Entering the Kingdom, The Soul's Great Need, The Competitive Laws and the Law of Love, The Finding of a Principle, At Rest in the Kingdom, The Heavenly Life, The Divine Center, The Eternal Now, "The Original Simplicity", The Unfailing Wisdom, The Might of Meekness, The Righteous Man, Perfect Love, Greatness and Goodness, and Heaven in the Heart.

AS A MAN THINKETH by James Allen. Thought and Character, Effect of Thought on Circumstances, Effect of Thought on Health and the Body, Thought and Purpose, The Thought-Factor in Achievement, Visions and Ideals, Serenity.

BYWAYS OF BLESSEDNESS by James Allen. Right Beginnings, Small Tasks and Duties, Transcending Difficulties and Perplexities, Burden-Dropping, Hidden Sacrifices, Sympathy, Forgiveness, Seeing No Evil, Abiding Joy, Silentness, Solitude, Standing Alone, Understanding the Simple Laws of Life, Happy Endings.

EIGHT PILLARS OF PROSPERITY by James Allen. Discussion on Energy, Economy, Integrity, Systems, Sympathy, Sincerity, Impartiality, Self-reliance, and the Temple of Prosperity

ENTERING THE KINGDOM by James Allen. The Soul's Great Need, The Competitive Laws and the Laws of Love, The Finding of a Principle, At Rest in the Kingdom, And All Things Added.

FROM PASSION TO PEACE by James Allen. Passion, Aspiration, Temptation, Transmutation, Transcendence, Beatitude, Peace.

FROM POVERTY TO POWER by James Allen. (Author of "As a Man Thinketh") Two books in one: The Path to Prosperity including World a Reflex of Mental States, The Way Out of Undesirable Conditions, Silent Power of Thought, Controlling and Directing One's Forces, The Secret of Health, Success, and Power, Etc. and The Way of Peace including Power of Meditation, The Two Masters, Self and Truth, The Acquirement of Spiritual Power, Realization of Selfless Love, Entering into the Infinite, Perfect Peace, Etc.

THE HEAVENLY LIFE by James Allen. The Divine Center, The Eternal Now, The "Original Simplicity", The Unfailing Wisdom, The Might of Meekness, The Righteous Man, Perfect Love, Perfect Freedom, Greatness and Goodness, Heaven in the Heart.

THE LIFE TRIUMPHANT by James Allen. Faith and Courage, Manliness and Sincerity, Energy and Power, Self-Control and Happiness, Simplicity and Freedom, Right-Thinking and Repose, Calmness and Resource, Insight and Nobility, Man and the Master, and Knowledge and Victory.

LIGHT ON LIFE'S DIFFICULTIES by James Allen. The Light that Leads to Perfect Peace, Light on Facts and Hypotheses, The Law of Cause and Effect in Human Life, Values - Spiritual and Material, The Sense of Proportion, Adherence to Principle, The Sacrifice of the Self, The Management of the Mind, Self-Control: The Door of Heaven, Acts and their Consequences, The Way of Wisdom, Disposition, Individual Liberty, The Blessing and Dignity of Work, Good Manner and Refinement, Diversity of Creeds, Law and Miracle, War and Peace, The Brotherhood of Man, Life's Sorrows, Life's Change, The Truth of Transitoriness, The Light that Never Goes Out.

MAN: KING OF MIND, BODY AND CIRCUMSTANCE by James Allen. The Inner World of Thoughts, The Outer World of Things, Habit: Its Slavery and Its Freedom, Bodily Conditions, Poverty, Man's Spiritual Dominion, Conquest: Not Resignation.

THE MASTERY OF DESTINY by James Allen. Deeds, Character, and Destiny, The Science of Self-Control, Cause and Effect in Human Conduct, Training of the Will, Thoroughness, Mind-Building and Life-Building, Cultivation of Concentration, Practice of Meditation, The Power of Purpose, The Joy of Accomplishment.

MEDITATIONS, A YEAR BOOK by James Allen. "James Allen may truly be called the Prophet of Meditation. In an age of strife, hurry, religious controversy, heated arguments, ritual and ceremony, he came with his message of Meditation, calling men away from the din and strife of tongues into the peaceful paths of stillness within their own souls, where 'the Light that lighteth every man that cometh into the world' ever burns steadily and surely for all who will turn their weary eyes from the strife without to the quiet within." Contains two quotes and a brief commentary for each day of the year.

MORNING AND EVENING THOUGHTS by James Allen. Contains a separate and brief paragraph for each morning and evening of the month.

OUT FROM THE HEART by James Allen. The Heart and the Life, The Nature of Power of Mind, Formation of Habit, Doing and Knowing, First Steps in the Higher Life, Mental Conditions and Their Effects, Exhortation.

THROUGH THE GATE OF GOOD by James Allen. The Gate and the Way, The Law and the Prophets, The Yoke and the Burden, The Word and the Doer, The Vine and the Branches, Salvation this Day.

THE WAY OF PEACE by James Allen. The Power of Meditation, The Two Masters: Self and Truth, The Acquirement of Spiritual Power, The Realization of Selfless Love, Entering into the Infinite, Saints, Sages, and Saviors, The Law of Service, The Realization of Perfect Peace.

PERSONALITY: ITS CULTIVATION AND POWER AND HOW TO ATTAIN by Lily L. Allen. Personality, Right Belief, Self-Knowledge, Intuition, Decision and Promptness, Self-Trust, Thoroughness, Manners, Physical Culture, Mental, Moral, and Spiritual Culture, Introspection, Emancipation, Self-Development, Self-Control and Mental

Poise, Liberty, Transformation, Balance, Meditation and Concentration.

KUNDALINI

AND THE SUN IS UP: KUNDALINI RISES IN THE WEST by W. Thomas Wolfe. Chapters include: The Hindu's View, The Esoteric Christian's View, The Professional Specialist's View, The Kundalini Subject's View, Physiological Effects, Spiritual Weightlessness, Emotional and Attitudinal Changes, Changed Dream Content, Event Control, The Reason for Summoning Up the Kundalini, Christ and the Kundalini, A Modern Parallel to the Second Coming, Etc.

LIGHT

PHILOSOPHY OF LIGHT – AN INTRODUCTORY TREATISE by Floyd Irving Lorbeer. The Ocean of Light, Sight and Light, Light and Perception, Some Cosmic Considerations, Light and Health, Electrical Hypothesis, Temperament, Beauty, and Love and Light, The Problem of Space and Time, Unity and Diversity, Deity, Soul, and Immortality, Light and the New Era, Etc.

PRINCIPLES OF LIGHT AND COLOR by Edwin D. Babbitt. (Illustrated, Complete 576p. version.) The Harmonic Laws of the Universe, The Etherio-Atomic Philosophy of Force, Chromo Chemistry, Chromo Therapeutics, and the General Philosophy of Finer Forces, Together with Numerous Discoveries and Practical Applications, Etc!

LONGEVITY

FOREVER YOUNG: HOW TO ATTAIN LONGEVITY by Gladys Iris Clark. Chapter include: Ageless Symbology, Followers of Fallen Luminaries, Rejuvenation Practices, Youth in Age-Old Wisdom, Angelic Travel Guides, Longevity Begins with God Awareness, Coping with Realities, Non-Aging Techniques in Action, Musing on Transition, Cancel Out Negatives, Grecian Nostalgia, Sedona's Seven Vortices, Crystals, Etc.

MEDITATION

CONCENTRATION AND MEDITATION by Christmas Humphreys. The Importance of Right Motive, Power of Thought, Dangers and Safeguards, Particular Exercises, Time, Place, Posture, Relaxation, Breathing, Thoughts, Counting the Breaths, Visualization and Color, Stillness, Motive, Self Analogy, Higher Meditation, The Voice of Mysticism, Jhanas, Zen, Satori, Koan, Ceremonial Magic, Taoism, Occultism, Mysticism, Theosophy, Yoga, The Noble Eightfold Path, Etc.

NEW AGE

THE MESSAGE OF AQUARIA by Curtiss. The Mystic Life, The Sign Aquarius, Are These the Last Days?, Comets and Eclipses, Law of Growth, Birth of the New Age, Mastery and the Masters of Wisdom, Mother Earth and the Four Winds, The Spiral of Life and Life Waves, The Message of the Sphinx, Day of Judgement and Law of Sacrifice, The Spiritual Birth, The True Priesthood, Etc.

NUMEROLOGY

NAMES, DATES, AND NUMBERS – A SYSTEM OF NUMEROLOGY by Roy Page Walton. The Law of Numbers, The Character and Influence of the Numbers, Application and Use of Numbers, Strong and Weak Names. The Number that Governs the Life, How Each Single Name Effects the Life, The Importance of Varying the Signature, How the Name Discloses the Future, Choosing a Suitable Name for a Child, Names Suitable for Marriage, How to Find Lucky Days and Months, Points to Bear in Mind.

NUMBERS: THEIR OCCULT POWER AND MYSTIC VIRTUE by W. Wynn Wescott. Pythagoras, His Tenets and His Followers, Pythagorean Views of Numbers, Kabalistic View on Numbers, Properties of the Numbers according to the Bible, the Talmuds, the Pythagoreans, the Romans, Chaldeans, Egyptians, Hindoos, Medieval Magicians, Hermetic Students, and the Rosicurcians.

NUMBER VIBRATION IN QUESTIONS AND ANSWERS by Mrs. L. Dow Balliett. Selections include: When Was Your First Birth?, The First Step in Reading a Name, Can the Name be Changed?, What Does the Birth Path Show?, The Numerical and Number Chart, Is an Esoteric Value to be Found in Gems?, Why Do We Not Add Either 22 or 11?, The Day of Reincarnation, Is Anybody Out of Place?, Are We Gods?, Of What Use is Prayer?, What is the Soul?, Should Rooms be Furnished in our Own Colors?, What Months Are Best for Creation?, What is Astral Music?, Where Should We Live?, Etc. Etc. Etc!

NUMERAL PHILOSOPHY by Albert Christy. A Study of Numeral Influences upon the Physical, Mental, and Spiritual Nature of Mankind.

VIBRATION: A SYSTEM OF NUMBERS AS TAUGHT BY PYTHARGORAS by Mrs. L. Dow Balliett. Chapters include: The Principles of Vibration, Numbers in Detail, What Your Name Means (broadly speaking), Business, Choosing A Husband or Wife, Pythagoras' Laws, Your Colors, Body Parts, Gems, Minerals, Flowers, Birds, Odors, Music, Guardian Angel, Symbols, Etc.

ORIENTAL (Also see "YOGA")

THE BUDDHA'S GOLDEN PATH by Dwight Goddard. Prince Siddhartha Gautama, Right Ideas, Speech, Behaviour, Right Vocation, Words, Conduct, Mindfulness, Concentration, Resolution, Environment, Intuition, Vows, Radiation, Spiritual Behaviour, Spirit, Etc.

BUSHIDO: WAY OF THE SAMURAI Translated from the classic Hagakure by Minoru Tanaka. This unique translation of a most important Japanese classic offers an explanation of the central and upright character of the Japanese people, and their indomitable inner strength. "The Way of the Samurai" is essential for businessmen, lawyers, students, or anyone who would understand the Japanese psyche.

DAO DE JING (LAO-ZI): THE OLD SAGE'S CLASSIC OF THE WAY OF VIRTUE translated by Patrick Michael Byrne. A new translation, faithful to both the letter and the poetic spirit of the original, of the ancient Chinese book of wisdom (traditionally known as the *Tao Te Ching* of Lao Tse or Lao Tsu: this version employs the new, more accurate *pinyin* transliteration). With introduction, notes and commentary.

FUSANG or THE DISCOVERY OF AMERICA BY CHINESE BUDDHIST PRIESTS IN THE FIFTH CENTURY by Charles G. Leland. Chinese Knowledge of Lands and Nations, The Road to America, The Kingdom of Fusang or Mexico, Of Writing and Civil Regulations in Fusang, Laws and Customs of the Aztecs, The Future of Eastern Asia, Travels of Other Buddhist Priests, Affinities of American and Asiatic Languages, Images of Buddha, Etc.

THE HISTORY OF BUDDHIST THOUGHT by Edward J. Thomas. The Ascetic Ideal, Early Doctrine: Yoga, Brahminism and the Upanishads, Karma, Release and Nirvana, Buddha, Popular Bodhisattva Doctrine, Buddhism and Modern Thought, Etc.

SACRED BOOKS OF THE EAST by Epiphanius Wilson. Vedic Hymns, The Zend-Avesta, The Dhammapada, The Upanishads, Selections from the Koran, Life of Buddha, Etc.

THE WISDOM OF THE HINDUS by Brian Brown. Brahmanic Wisdom, Maha-Bharata, The Ramayana, Wisdom of the Upanishads, Vivekananda and Ramakrishna on Yoga Philosophy, Wisdom of Tuka-Ram, Paramananda, Vivekananda, Abbedananda, Etc.

PALMISTRY

INDIAN PALMISTRY by Mrs. J.B. Dale. A Summary of Judgement, Signification of Animals, Flowers, and Promiscuous Marks Found on the Hand, The Lines, The Mounts, The Line of Life, The Events, The Line of the Head and Brain, The Line of Fortune, Saturn, Venus and Mars, The Rule to Tell The Planets, The Mount of Jupiter, Apollo the Sun, The Moon, The Mount of Saturn, The Planet Mercury, Mensa: The Part of Fortune, The Fingers and Thumb, The Head and Signs of the Feet, The Arms, Etc.

PHILOSOPHY

GOETHE – WITH SPECIAL CONSIDERATION OF HIS PHILOSOPHY by Paul Carus. The Life of Goethe, His Relation to Women, Goethe's Personality, The Religion of Goethe, Goethe's Philosophy, Literature and Criticism, The Significance of "Faust", Miscellaneous Epigrams and Poems. (Heavily Illustrated).

PROPHECY (Also See Earth Changes)

THE STORY OF PROPHECY by Henry James Forman. What is Prophecy?, Oracles, The Great Pyramid Speaks, The End of the Age: Biblical Prophecy, Medieval Prophecy, Astrologers and Saints, Prophecies Concerning the Popes, Nostradamus, America In Prophecy, The Prophetic Future.

PYRAMIDOLOGY

THE GREAT PYRAMID. Two Essays plus illustrations, one from The Reminder and the other from J.F. Rowney Press. Selections include: The Pyramid's Location and Constructional Features, Some of the Pyramid's Scientific Features, other Features of the Great Pyramid, Complete History of Mankind Represented in the Pyramid, The Shortening of Time, The Symbolism of the Passages and Chambers, Etc.

THE GREAT PYRAMID - Its Construction, Symbolism, and Chronology by Basil Stewart. Construction and Astrological Features, Chart of World History, Missing Apex-stone, Who Built It? Plus Various Diagrams.

REINCARNATION

LIFE AFTER LIFE: THE THEORY OF REINCARNATION by Eustace Miles. Have We Lived Before? Questions Often Asked, Does Not Oppose Christianity, Great Men Who Have Believed, etc.

THE NEW REVELATION by Sir Arthur Conan Doyle. The Search, The Revelation, The Coming Life, Problems and Limitations, The Next Phase of Life, Automatic Writing, The Cheriton Dugout.

REINCARNATION by George B. Brownell. He Knew Who He Was, Memories of Past Lives, A Remarkable Proof, Lived Many Lives, An Arabian Incarnation, Dreamed of Past Life, Great Minds and Reincarnation, The Bible and Reincarnation, Karma, Atlantis Reborn, Thought is Destiny, The Celestial Body, The Hereafter, Etc.

REINCARNATION by Katherine Tingley. What Reincarnation Is, Arguments for Reincarnation, Supposed Objections to Reincarnation, Reincarnation and Heredity, Reincarnation in Antiquity, Reincarnation the Master-Key to Modern Problems, Reincarnation in Modern Literature.

THE RING OF RETURN by Eva Martin. Pre-Christian Era, Early Christian and Other Writings of the First Five Centuries A.D., Miscellaneous Sources Before A.D. 1700, A.D. 1700-1900, The Twentieth Century. In this book, Miss Eva Martin has brought together a most complete and scholarly collection of references to past, present, and future life.

RELIGIONS

THE BIBLE IN INDIA - HINDOO ORIGIN OF HEBREW AND CHRISTIAN REVELATION Translated from "La Bible Dans L'Inde" by Louis Jacolliot. India's Relation to Antiquity, Manou, Manes, Minos, Moses, What the Lessons of History are Worth, Brahminical Perversions of Primitive Vedism, Virgins of the Pagodas and Rome, Moses or Moise and Hebrew Society, Zeus - Jezeus - Isis - Jesus, Moses Founds Hebrew Society on the Model of Egypt and India, The Hindoo Genesis, Zeus and Brahma, Devas and Angels, The Hindoo Trinity, Adima (In Sanscrit, The First Man), Ceylon as the Garden of Paradise, The Woman of the Vedas and The Woman of the Bible, The Deluge According to the Maha-Barata, Prophecies Announcing the Coming of Christna, Birth of the Virgin Devanaguy, Massacre of all Male Children Born on the Same Night as Christna, Christna Begins to Preach the New Law, His Disciples,

14

Parable of the Fisherman, Christna's Philosophic Teaching, Transfiguration of Christna, His Disiples Give Him The Name of Jezeus (Pure Essence), Christna and the Two Holy Women, Death of Christna, Hindoo Origin of the Christian Idea, Devanaguy and Mary, Christna and Christ, Massacre of the Innocents in India and Judea, Hindoo and Christian Transfiguration, Apocrypha of St. John, Whence the Monks and Hermits of Primitive Christianity, A Text of Manou, Etc!

NATURAL LAW IN THE SPIRITUAL WORLD by Henry Drummond. Biogenesis, Degeneration, Growth, Death, Mortification, Eternal Life, Environment, Conformity to Type, Semi-Parasitism, Parasitism, Classification.

PRINCIPAL SYMBOLS OF WORLD RELIGIONS by Swami Harshananda. Chapters include discussions of the symbols of these religions: Hinduism, Buddhism, Jainism, Sikhism, Shintoism, Islam, Christianity, Judaism, Zoroastrianism, Taoism.

THE RELIGION OF THE SIKH GURUS by Teja Singh, M.A., Teja Singh, formerly a professor of history at Khalsa College in Amritsar, outlines the foundation of history, tradition, ritual and principles which has kept disciples of the the Sikh religion strong and united into the present day.

SELF-HELP / RECOVERY (See under "Inspiration, etc.")

SOUL

THE HUMAN SOUL IN SLEEPING, DREAMING AND WAKING by F.W. Zeylmans van Emmichoven, M.D. Featured subjects include: What is the Soul?, How, by observing the phenomena of life, we can find the reality of the soul and its connections with the human organism. Man as a threefold being. Dreams. Psycho-Analysis. The awakening of the soul. Fears. Meditation, Concentration and Self Development. The counterforces that work against man's spiritual striving. Spiritual Science as a psychology of the living, developing soul, Etc.

TAROT

THE ILLUSTRATED KEY TO THE TAROT – THE VEIL OF DIVINATION by Arthur Edward Waite. The Veil and Its Symbols, The Tarot in History, The Doctrine Behind the Veil, The Outer Method of the Oracles, The Four Suits of Tarot Cards, The Art of Tarot Divination, An Ancient Celtic Method of Divination.

THE KEY OF DESTINY by H.A. and F.H. Curtiss. The Initiate, Twelve-fold Division of the Zodiac, Reincarnation and Transmutation, The Solar System, The Letters of the Tarot, The Numbers 11 thru 22, Twelve Tribes and Twelve Disciples, The Great Work, The Labors of Hercules, Necromancy, Great Deep, Temperance, Man the Creator vs. the Devil, Celestial Hierarchies, The New Jerusalem, Etc.

THE KEY TO THE UNIVERSE by H.A. and F.H. Curtiss. Origin of the Numerical Systems, Symbols of the "O" as the Egg and the Cat, The "O" as the Aura and the Ring Pass Not, Symbol of the O, Letters of the Tarot, The Numbers 1 thru 10, The 7 Principles of Man, The 7 Pleiades and the 7 Rishis, Joy of Completion.

WESTERN MYSTICISM

BROTHERHOOD OF MT. SHASTA by Eugene E. Thomas. From Clouds to Sunshine, Finding the Brotherhood, The Lake of Gold, The Initiation, Memories of the Past, In Advance of the Future, Prodigy, Trial, and Visitor, The Annihilation and the King, The Lost Lemuria.

THE ELEUSINIAN MYSTERIES AND RITES by Dudley Wright. Preface, Introduction, The Eleusinian Legend, The Ritual of the Mysteries, Program of the Greater Mysteries, The Intimate Rites, The Mystical Significance, Bibliography.

KALEVALA: THE LAND OF THE HEROES Translated by W. F. Kirby. The National Epic of Finland. "...the Kalevala itself could one day becomes as important for all of humanity as Homer was for the Greeks."

MYRIAM AND THE MYSTIC BROTHERHOOD by Maude Lesseuer Howard. A novel in the western mystic tradition.

THE WAY OF ATTAINMENT by Sydney T. Klein. The Invisible is the Real, The Power of Prayer, Spiritual Regeneration, Dogma of the Virgin Birth, Finding the Kingdom of Heaven "Within", Realizing Oneness with God, Nature of the Ascent, Reaching the Summit.

THE WAY OF MYSTICISM by Joseph James. God Turns Towards Man, The Unexpected, The Still Small Voice, His Exceeding Brightness, Man Turns Towards God, The Obstructive "Me", Where East and West Unite, Beside the Still Waters, Love's Meeting Place, Work – A Prayer, Every Pilgrim's Progress, Love's Fulfillment.

TABLOID MAGAZINE The Astral Projection. Metaphysical Tabloid Magazine from the early 1970's. Last three issues available.

YOGA (also see ORIENTAL)

YOGA PHILOSOPHY AND PRACTICE by Hari Prasad Shastri. The History and Literature of Yoga, The Epics and Bhagavad Gita, Patanjali, Shankaracharya, The Philosophy of Yoga, The Vedanta, Reason and Intuition, The Teacher (Guru), Advita (Non-Dualism), God and the World, God (Brahman) and the Individual (Jiva), The Nature of the Self, The Personal God (Ishvara), Three Views of Maya, The Three Gunas, Ethics, Action (Karma), Death and Reincarnation, Liberation, The Practice of Yoga, Subjects for Meditation, Peace of Mind, The True Self, Dream and Sleep, Vital Currents of the Body, OM, Practice in Daily Life, Austerity, Posture, Pranayama (Control of the Vital Currents), Concentration, Contemplation (Dhyana), Samadhi, Liberation in Life, Practical Program, Obstructions, Common Sense in Training, The Process in Brief, Three Yogis, Rama Tirtha, Shri Dada, Kobo Daishi, Illustrative Passages from the Literature of Yoga, Prayers from the Vedas, The Upanishads, The Bhagavad Gita, Yoga Vasishtha, The Ashtavakra Gita, Poem by Swami Rama Tirtha, Glossary, Etc!

GENERAL NON-METAPHYSICAL

BEST ENGRAVINGS by Skip Whitson. One hundred twenty three beautiful steel cut and wood cut engravings from the nineteenth century.

BUSTED IN MEXICO by Ann Palmer and Jessica Herman. One young woman's story of the devastating effects of the loss of liberty. A True Story, Introduction by Governor Jerry Apodaca.

THE LAND OF ENCHANTMENT FROM PIKE'S PEAK TO THE PACIFIC by Lilian Whiting. Chapters include: With Western Stars and Sunsets, Denver the Beautiful, The Picturesque Region of Pike's Peak, Summer Wanderings in Colorado, The Colorado Pioneers, The Surprises of New Mexico, The Story of Santa Fe, Magic and Mystery of Arizona, The Petrified Forest and the Meteorite Mountain, Los Angeles, The Spell-Binder, Grand Canyon, the Carnival of the Gods.

SUN HISTORICAL SERIES 33 titles ranging from Maine 100 years ago to Hawaii 100 years ago.

MAYDAYS AND MERMAIDS by William A. Davis. A contemporary tale of the sea. Vivid fast moving satirical yarn, spun on the paradoxical spool of tragicomedy. "Once you start this book there is a high probability that you will not put it down." - Clark Chambers, Critic.

For a PRICE LIST of all currently available Sun Books titles write: Book List, Sun Publishing Co., P.O. Box 5588, Santa Fe, NM 87502-5588